THE TRUE GRACE OF GOD

this is the true grace of God in which you stand.
1Peter 5:12
by

George Sidney Hurd

All texts are quoted from the New King James Version unless otherwise indicated.
Other versions cited from are listed below with their abbreviations:

ASV   American Standard Version
CLV   Concordant Literal Version
Darby   Darby Bible 1889
EPT   The New Testament: An Expanded Translation by Kenneth S. Wuest
ESV   English Standard Version
HCS   Holman Christian Standard Bible
KJV   King James Version
NASU   New American Standard Updated Edition
NIV   New International Version
NRSV   New Revised Standard Version
MKJV   Modern King James Version
PLT   Personal Literal Translation
TEV   Today's English Version
YLT   Young's Literal Translation

Contents

Acknowledgments

I am truly grateful to my dear wife, Norma who has shared the same vision and has always supported me in spite of having to sacrifice so much as I dedicated myself to writing. Also, my daughter Monica has been a tremendous help with the proofreading of my Spanish translations.

I am especially indebted to my dear friends Paul and Betty Wetselaar, who have shared the spiritual journey with me since the beginning of our walk with the Lord in the '60s. They have greatly assisted me in editing all of my books.

INTRODUCTION

As the forgiven slave trader, John Newton, expressed over two hundred years ago in his timeless hymn, "Amazing Grace," the true grace of God is wonderful and amazing, far beyond our feeble abilities to comprehend, let alone describe with mere words. The song has found a place in the hearts of millions worldwide due to mankind's inner longing for unmerited acceptance. Once unveiled to our understanding, the true grace of God transforms not only our approach to God but our daily walk as well.

Grace is much more than the Father's initial embrace of His unworthy prodigal sons - It is a continual supply for all our needs according to the inexhaustible riches of His grace in Christ Jesus. Jesus Christ is the embodiment of grace, and through the new birth we actually become one spirit with Him *(John 1:14-17; 1Cor 6:17).* Through this union with Christ everything that He is we have now become. Everything that He possesses we possess. Through this union with Him we have His perfect righteousness. We have His wisdom or the mind of Christ. We have His sanctification *(1Cor 1:30).*

By grace, through His life in us, we are now being renewed in our minds and hearts into His own image and likeness day by day. Also, it is by grace that the works which the Father foreordained for us are lived out in us by Christ who is now our very life.

As the song "Amazing Grace" declares, it is His amazing grace from beginning to end for His elect children. The stanza says: *"Tis grace that brought us safe thus far, and grace will lead us home."* I chose as the title for this book *"The True Grace of God,"* taken from Peter's first epistle because in his epistle he demonstrates how the true grace of God both initiates and perfects our salvation. From the beginning to the end it is by His grace and for His glory. In the first chapter he demonstrates how it is the grace of God from the very beginning:

"Peter, an apostle of Jesus Christ, to the pilgrims of the Dispersion in Pontus, Galatia, Cappadocia, Asia, and Bithynia, 2 **elect according to the foreknowledge of God the Father,** *in sanctification of the Spirit, for obedience and sprinkling of the blood of Jesus Christ: Grace to you and peace be multiplied. 3*

Blessed be the God and Father of our Lord Jesus Christ, who according to His abundant mercy has begotten us again to a living hope through the resurrection of Jesus Christ from the dead, 4 to an inheritance incorruptible and undefiled and that does not fade away, reserved in heaven for you, 5 who are kept by the power of God through faith for salvation ready to be revealed in the last time." (1Peter 1:1-5)

From the very beginning Peter declares that our election was according to His *foreknowledge*. The word translated *"foreknowledge"* does not simply mean "to know beforehand." The Greek word *prognosis* speaks of intimacy. Based upon His foreknowledge and His mercy He caused us to be born again to an *incorruptible* inheritance, reserved in heaven for us. Peter continues saying that we are kept by His power for a salvation which will be revealed in the Second Coming of Christ. At the close of his epistle, Peter summarizes it all for us with these words:

*"But may **the God of all grace**, who called us to His eternal glory by Christ Jesus, **after you have suffered a while,** ("will **Himself**" Gr. autos) **perfect, establish, strengthen, and settle you**. 11 **To Him be the glory** and the dominion forever and ever. Amen. 12 By Silvanus, our faithful brother as I consider him, I have written to you briefly, exhorting and testifying that **this is the true grace of God** in which you stand." (1Peter 5:10-12)*

This is the true grace of God. As I hope to demonstrate in this book, any understanding of grace that falls short of the grace of God here described by Peter is a falling short of the true grace of God. For centuries the concept of grace presented to the Church from most pulpits has been a false, flesh-empowering, mixed-grace message. The result has been that many who began well in the pure grace of God at initial salvation fall from the true grace into a *grace plus works acceptance mentality*. This version of grace has reduced the grace of God, making it out to be nothing more than a turbo-charger added on to our flesh-engine, empowering our flesh to finish the work which Christ began in us.

This false, humanistic version of grace has converted the Christian walk into a virtual nightmare for many sincere, sensitive children of God - especially those who realize that in their flesh they are *foolish, weak and ordinary,* which would include most of us *(1Cor 1:26-29).* The self-sufficient, who are strong in their own eyes, actually prefer the turbo-charged version of grace because it seems manageable for them and it makes them look good compared to their brethren who are weaker in the flesh. But for the great majority of the elect of God, who are consciously aware that their flesh-engine is burned out, this turbo-charged add-on to their flesh-engine is of no real benefit. This version of grace is more useless to them than king Saul's armor was to David when confronting Goliath.

This distorted version of grace has driven many with hearts like that of David to despair. They received a new heart after God's own heart upon receiving Christ, only to find that religion had dressed them in an armor that hinders, rather than empowers them. Many who began well have become discouraged and thrown in the towel, going back into the world. But others out of deep anguish of soul are now rediscovering the *true grace of God.* This has given rise to what has become known to some as the "Grace Revolution," or "The Grace Movement."

Listening to the testimonies of many of the leading voices in this grace movement, one can see that it is a movement which was born out of their great despair of trying to live out a traditional graceless Christianity, and their new discoveries have led to a new freedom from the power of sin and a new confidence to come boldly before the throne of grace to receive freely all that Christ obtained for them through His death and resurrection. They are rediscovering the truth that all the promises of God really are yes and amen in Christ Jesus our Lord. They share how obedience and good works are no longer seen by them as a means of obtaining God's acceptance, but rather the fruit of living in the assurance of God's acceptance of them by grace. They have found a new rest in the knowledge that Jesus now lives out His own righteousness in them and works through them as they simply abide in Him.

Their opponents take them to task when they describe their new life in grace as an "effortless Christianity" and cite Scriptures which *could* be construed in such a way as to prove them wrong. We will examine those Scriptures in their context at a later time, but didn't Jesus say: "My yoke is easy and my burden is light?" Could it just be possible that *striving in the grace of God* and *fleshly striving* are poles apart? There is a world of difference between *striving in the flesh* and *"striving according to His working which works in me mightily." (Col 1:29).*

9

Admittedly, this rediscovery of the grace of God, as with any new movement, has some excesses and abuses, and unfortunately the whole movement has been stigmatized by some opponents who refer to it as the "Hyper-Grace Movement" or "The Modern Grace Movement" and the entire movement is being categorized by some as being part of the end-time apostasy. They may be correct in saying that some on the outer fringe of the movement are in danger of this because they go too far, turning the grace of God into a license for immorality *(Jude 4),* but it is unfair to categorize the entire movement by a minority.

It would be good to see leaders within the Body of Christ who are divided on this vital subject come together and objectively compare notes, examining them in the light of the overall teaching of Scripture on the subject of grace. There is a need for humility on both sides, making a sincere effort to come to a unity of understanding concerning grace. While every doctrine of Scripture is indispensable for life and godliness, no other doctrine of Scripture is of such great import as is the true grace of God. We can perhaps tolerate differences concerning end-time chronology, or even between Calvinism, Arminianism or Biblical Universalism, but if we fall short of the grace of God we become like a ship at sea without a sail, or like a man trying to go upriver without a paddle. That is why the Scriptures tell us that we must stand upon *the true grace of God* and be *established by it;* we must *continue in grace, grow in grace* and *be strong in grace (1Peter 5:12; Heb 13:9; Acts 13:43; 2Peter 3:18).* We must be careful to not be turned away from the gospel of the grace of Christ unto another "gospel" which, according to Paul, is in reality not the gospel of grace at all, but rather a perversion of it *(Gal 1:6-9).*

Some time ago, I determined to seek the Lord for clarity on this all-important subject. I sought to objectively consider the arguments from both sides of the grace teaching. I read and reread all the books and watched the teaching videos available to me on the subject from both camps. However, in spite of convincing arguments from both sides, they all often left me asking: "but if that is so, then what about such and such a verse?"

Many of the leaders, especially among those of the grace movement, avoid altogether any mention of numerous texts in the New Testament, including the epistles, which seem to contradict certain elements of their grace doctrine. When they do attempt to reconcile those problem texts to their doctrine of grace, they often create more questions than answers. The grace opponents, on the other hand, often seem to miss the import of certain texts and are often so reactionary that they put themselves at risk of falling short of the true grace of God in order to counter what they see as excesses within the grace movement.

However, not all the fears of the opponents of the grace movement are unfounded. The true grace of God is the straight and narrow path that few saints walk upon. Ever since Adam and Eve partook of the tree of the knowledge of good and evil the majority of us continue to partake of the forbidden fruit rather than depending entirely upon God. The religiously self-righteous, who partake of the forbidden fruit from the good branches, trust in their own righteousness and see the grace of God as being nothing more than a booster to their own self-efforts. On the other hand, those who consistently partake of the fruit from the evil branches, often, rather than repenting and receiving the true grace of God for cleansing and transformation, redefine the grace of God into nothing more than a permissive embrace from an overly consenting Father who never intervenes to correct His children. They present the Father as though He were perfectly pleased with them at all times, no matter what sins they may be into.

A danger, which the critics of the grace movement must guard against, is finding themselves perched on a "good branch" of the forbidden tree, crying *foul* to those who are partaking of the evil branches of the same tree in the name of grace. The truth is that both branches are laden with forbidden, toxic fruit - one producing self-righteousness and the other self-indulgence. For either of them to say that they are in the grace of God would be self-delusion. What they call grace would in reality be a false grace and not the true grace of God. The true grace of God is found in the person of Jesus. The straight and narrow grace walk is nothing less than Jesus Himself, the Way, the Truth and the Life. To abide in Him is to abide in the true grace.

My journey through this amazing theme of grace has been at times unsettling and even frightening for fear of misinterpreting God's revelation of Himself. Exposing oneself to two opposing points of view concerning God's heart of grace is to tread on holy ground and I do not do it lightly. It can be quite disconcerting to plow up one's own theological field in both directions in order to uproot a mixed crop

11

and undertake the laborious task of replanting it with the pure seed of God's Word alone. If that is where you are on this subject, I invite you to join with me as I attempt to share with you some of my discoveries concerning what I see as the true grace of God.

Chapter one
The New has come

Our sufficiency is from God,
Who also made us sufficient as ministers of the new covenant,
Not of the letter but of the Spirit;
For the letter kills, but the Spirit gives life.
2Corinthians 3:5b,6

Throughout the New Testament we see a contrast made between the Old Covenant and the New Covenant that is as marked as night is from day or life from death. Even as far back as the times of the Prophets, God made it clear that the New Covenant He was going to make with His people would not be comparable with the Old Covenant He made with them at Sinai *(Jer 31:31-34; Ezek 36:26,27).*

Nevertheless, in spite of this obvious and marked contrast between the old and the new, announced by the Prophets and set forth clearly by Jesus and His apostles, most within the Church throughout the centuries have been fed a spiritually toxic mix which, to a greater or a lesser degree, has presented the New Covenant as being nothing more than a new and improved amended version of the old.

However, as we shall see, the Old Covenant - the Law of Moses, being given 430 years after the promise to Abraham, was only to remain in place until the promised Seed of Abraham should come, through whom ultimately all the families of the earth would be blessed, when He initiates an entirely New Covenant through His blood. In this New Covenant the Lord promised that He would give us a new heart and put His Spirit within us, causing us to walk in His ways. He promised that under this New Covenant relationship He would remember our sins no more. The stated purpose of the Law was to serve as a tutor for the people of God to bring them to Christ. Therefore, upon initiating the New Covenant, Paul declares that we are no longer under the tutor – the Law *(Gal 3:25).*

Contrasts between the Old Covenant of Law and the New Covenant of Grace

In various occasions and in different ways the Scriptures make a clear-cut contrast between the Old Covenant of Law and the New Covenant of Grace. Many of these contrasts make it clear that any mixture of law and grace nullifies the benefits of the New Covenant of Grace in our daily walk *(Gal 2:21 NAS)*. As early as Jeremiah, the Lord made it clear that the new would not be comparable to the old:

> *"The time is coming, declares the Lord, when I will make a new covenant with the house of Israel and with the house of Judah. 32* ***It will not be like*** *the covenant I made with their forefathers when I took them by the hand to lead them out of Egypt..." (Jer 31:31-32 NIV)*

The Old was God at a Distance – The New is God in us

> *"For the law **was given** through Moses, but grace and truth **came** (sing.) through Jesus Christ." (John 1:17)*

The glorious contrast that John makes here between the Old Covenant of Law and the New Covenant of Grace is that God remained at a distance from the moment He gave the Law, whereas He actually *came* in the person of Jesus Christ, being full of grace and truth. Paul says that God did not give the Law in person to Israel, but rather that it was ordained by angels in the hand of a mediator *(Gal 3:19)*. In contrast, Jesus himself initiated the New Covenant of Grace personally, shedding His own blood for us. It is important to note that *"came" is* not in plural, as though grace and truth were being presented as two things separate from the person of Jesus. The verb *"came"* is in singular, indicating that Jesus is himself the embodiment of grace and truth.

One prominent opponent of the grace teaching, taking advantage of the fact that the conjunction *"but"* in John 1:17 is in italics, (indicating that it is not in the original Greek text), tried to argue that we should supply instead the conjunction *"and"* which would make grace out to be an addition to the Law rather than something new and separate from it. However, the contrast between law and grace here is obvious, even without inserting the conjunction *"but."* The New Testament, on numerous occasions, makes this contrast

14

between law and grace. One example is *"For sin shall not have dominion over you, for **you are not under law __but__ under grace.**" (Rom 6:14).* He warned that those believers who return to the old regimen of the law have fallen from grace *(Gal 5:1-4).*

The Old brought Death – the New Gives us the Very Life of God

*"...our sufficiency is from God, 6 who also made us sufficient as ministers of the new covenant, not of the letter but of the Spirit; for **the letter kills**, but **the Spirit gives life**. 7 But if the **ministry of death, written and engraved on stones**, was glorious, so that the children of Israel could not look steadily at the face of Moses because of the glory of his countenance, which glory was passing away, 8 how will the ministry of the Spirit not be more glorious? 9 For if the **ministry of condemnation** had glory, the **ministry of righteousness** exceeds much more in glory. 10 For even what was made glorious had no glory in this respect, because of the glory that excels. 11 For if what is **passing away** was glorious, what **remains** is much more glorious." (2Cor 3:5-11)*

The Old Covenant Law was external - letters written on tablets of stone, and its only purpose was to bring death and condemnation to those under it. It promised life but only for perfect obedience. Since the law could not make anyone perfect due to the fact that it only revealed our sin instead of producing life and godliness, it resulted in those under it despairing of ever achieving the perfect righteousness which the Law required through their own self-efforts.

From its very inception, this was the divine intent in the giving of the Law of Moses. It was given to bring us to see our need for God's grace. It was our tutor to bring us to Christ. The Law was given that the transgression might *abound,* but now under Grace, His grace is that which *super-abounds* in us unto righteousness *(Rom 5:20).* God used the mirror of the Law to show our disobedience, but only in order to ultimately have mercy on us as soon as we acknowledge our need and look to Him for grace: *"For God has shut up all in unbelief, so that He might show mercy to all." (Rom 11:32 MKJV).* The Law ministers death to us but only in order that God might give us His own eternal life: *"For I through the law died to the law **that I might live to God**." (Gal 2:19).*

Whereas the Old Covenant Law was external, with God at a distance, under the New Covenant of Grace, God, in the person of Jesus Christ has now come to live out His own resurrection life in all those who, through the Law, have despaired of ever attaining to self-righteousness and receive Him.

Independence has been the root problem in man since Adam and Eve acted independently from God, partaking of the forbidden fruit. They thought it would make them more like God, but what it made man was a god unto himself, disconnected from His Creator and lost. God's purpose in giving the Law was to bring us to an end of ourselves that we might afterwards come back into union with Him through His grace. When we look away from ourselves and put our faith in Christ, we become one spirit with Him through the new birth. Our old self ceased to exist and having been born again, we are now a new creation in Him.

*"For what the law could not do in that it was weak through the flesh, God did by sending His own Son in the likeness of sinful flesh, on account of sin: He condemned sin in the flesh, 4 that the righteous requirement of the law might be **fulfilled in us** who do not walk according to the flesh but according to the Spirit." (Rom 8:3,4)*

We see then that the Law was given to reveal the inability of our old independent adamic flesh. It was given to reveal that the flesh truly profits nothing. God's solution wasn't to come to the aid of our independent flesh but to condemn and crucify it so that we may live unto Him. In the timing of the Father, the Son of God became incarnate in the likeness of sinful flesh, but without sin. As EMANUEL, "God with us," He showed us the Father, living a life of perfect dependence upon the Father. When He died in our place, He not only took away our sins, but the whole humanity of sinful flesh also died with Him - the adamic nature was also crucified with Him.

But it keeps getting better. He arose from the dead and ascended to the Father, sprinkling His own blood on the heavenly mercy seat, thereby perfecting forever those who are sanctified. And then the Father sent the Holy Spirit, according to the promise of the New Covenant:

*"I will give you **a new heart** and put **a new spirit** within you; I will take the heart of stone out of your flesh and give you a heart of*

*flesh. I will put **My Spirit within you** and cause you to walk in My statutes, and you will keep My judgments and do them....I will forgive their iniquity, and their sin I will remember no more." (Ezek 36:26,27; Jer 31:34b)*

Some advocates of the Law for New Covenant living draw attention to the mention here of His laws, statutes and judgments being kept by us under the New Covenant. However, we see that under the New Covenant we live by the Spirit, and as we simply walk according to the Holy Spirit, He himself produces the *righteous requirements* of the law through us. Under grace, they are fulfilled *in us* rather than *by us (Rom 8:4)*. Under the Law, the Jews were given a written list of the righteous requirements that *they* were to fulfill to the letter. It was a works righteousness regimen.

In contrast, we see that what we as believers produce when we walk in the Spirit, are not *works* but His *fruit*. That is why a Gentile believer with absolutely no knowledge of the Law of Moses can simply walk in the Spirit and the Holy Spirit will produce in him **His fruit** which is *"love, joy, peace, longsuffering, kindness, goodness, faithfulness, 23 gentleness, self-control. **Against such there is no law." (Gal 5:22-23)*. However, if a Jew were to ask that same Gentile believer if He was keeping the Law, he would reply: "What Law?"

We will answer the arguments for law-keeping under the New Covenant at a later time. But clearly, we can see that one contrast between the old and the new is that the Law was given to bring death to self-confidence in the old fleshly nature that we might look away to Jesus and receive new life in Him, in order that we might have His righteousness fulfilled *in us* by the Holy Spirit. *"For the letter kills, but the Spirit gives life." (2Cor 3:6)*. As Paul says, we are now under an entirely new regimen of life:

*"But now we have been delivered from the law, having died to what we were held by, so that **we should serve in the newness of the Spirit** and **not in the oldness of the letter**." (Rom 7:6)*

The Old Wineskins cannot contain the New Wine

"And no one puts new wine into old wineskins; or else the new wine will burst the wineskins and be spilled, and the wineskins will be ruined. But new wine must be put into new wineskins, and both are preserved." (Luke 5:37-38)

Although Jesus was born, lived and died under the Old Covenant Law and perfectly fulfilled it, during His final three-and-a-half year ministry He began to lay the ground-work for the New Covenant that He was about to initiate through His blood shed on the cross. For the religiously self-righteous, He raised the bar of the Law even higher, so that they would despair of salvation by their own works and seek the mercy of God. For those in self-despair, He extended grace and acceptance without any demands or reproaches. In reading the four gospels, it is very important to rightly divide the word of truth, carefully considering who Jesus was addressing in each context and what He was trying to get across to them. His words contain a mixture of the severity of the Old Covenant towards some, and the kindness and grace of the New towards others. When Jesus was alone with His disciples, He explained to them that, in order to understand His sayings, they had to learn to separate the old from the new. He said to them:

"Therefore every scribe instructed concerning the kingdom of heaven is like a householder who brings out of his treasure things new and old." (Matt 13:52)

In the parable of the wineskins, Jesus again refers to the new and the old. In the context, Jesus is confronting the inflexible legalism of the Pharisees, and at the same time He was teaching us something very important concerning the New Covenant He was about to initiate. To the discerning scribe of Jesus, His words are seen as a warning against trying to put the New Covenant of Grace within the confines of the Old Covenant of Law. The glory of the Christ of the New Covenant is much greater than that of Moses and the Old Covenant Law *(Heb 3:3; 2Cor 3:10,11)*. It is Christ's life in us that is the hope of glory - not law observance. To bolster that hope with Law-keeping is an affront to Christ. Paul makes this clear when He says:

"I do not nullify the grace of God, for if righteousness comes through the Law, then Christ died needlessly." (Gal 2:21 NAS)

If we try to pour the new wine of grace into the old wineskin of the Law, supplementing the grace of God with the works of the Law for righteousness, we nullify the grace of God and deny the sufficiency of Christ's death and the power of His resurrection life within us for our sanctification. It is an affront to the Holy Spirit of grace who is our Helper under the New Covenant and abides with us forever *(John*

18

14:16). As Paul says in Galatians 5:4, if we attempt to be justified by law, we have fallen from grace. And when he speaks of being justified by the law, he is not only referring to initial salvation. This is clear from Galatians 3, where he says:

> *"This only I want to learn from you: **Did you receive the Spirit by the works of the law,** or by the hearing of faith? 3 Are you so foolish? **Having begun in the Spirit, are you now being made perfect by the flesh?**" (Gal 3:2,3)*

In this passage, *"by the works of the law"* and *"by the flesh"* are interchangeable terms. What Paul is countering is the error that taught that, although we received the Spirit by grace, we will not be justified in the end if we do not sanctify ourselves through law observance. That amounts to confining the new wine of the New Covenant within the old wineskin of the Old Covenant. Sadly, that is what many Christians today believe that we must do. We must understand that we not only begin by the Spirit, without the works of the Law, but we are also being perfected by the Spirit, by grace, without the works of the Law. To seek perfection through Law observance is to fall from grace and must be repented of in order to allow the Spirit to continue conforming us to the image of Christ, who now lives in us.

Do Portions of the Old Covenant Law continue into the New?

Most opponents of the New Covenant teaching on grace only insist upon keeping a part of the Old Covenant Law. The majority would only insist upon Eleven Commandments (the Ten Commandments plus tithing). Most do not circumcise their children on the eighth day after birth. Most do not abide by the dietary restrictions of the Law, considering all meats to be clean and even clothing themselves with mixed fabrics. Most no longer observe the new moons and feast days, with the sounding of trumpets (although the shofar is now being heard again in some charismatic circles).

Many who think we must observe the Ten Commandments, including the Sabbath, meet on Sunday. But the Sabbath, under the Law, was from Friday sundown to Saturday sundown, and in order to keep it, they could not do any work, including the preparing of a meal. They could not buy or sell, or travel more than a Sabbath day's journey, which was only 2,000 paces, or less than a mile. The Sabbatarians, who still attempt to observe the true Jewish Sabbath to this day, boast in being the only ones who keep the entire Ten Commandments.

I was raised as a Seventh Day Adventist. They are very strict about Sabbath observance on the seventh day which is Saturday. In our home we had an Adventist calendar which indicated the exact time of the official sundown each Saturday for our region, and as soon as the clock marked the hour, we turned our radios and televisions back on. As an adolescent, I lived for a time in an Adventist College community, several miles from the nearest pagan town, and I remember the frustration of being a teenage rebel but not being able to buy gasoline because the only gas stations were closed from Friday sundown to Saturday sundown. Also, all stores and shops were closed for miles around, and even if they were open, no meat or junk foods were sold in the community's stores, and part of my rebellion was against imposed vegetarianism.

During the 2016 US presidential campaign one of my favorite candidates for the presidency was Dr. Ben Carson, but since he was a Seventh Day Adventist, I doubted he would be able to adequately defend our nation, since all our enemies would have known that the Oval Office would have been closed from sundown Friday to sundown Saturday while our president kept the Sabbath.

The New Testament is very clear in stating we are no longer under any part of the Old Covenant Law of Moses. For example, Paul in Romans seven begins by saying:

*"Therefore, my brethren, **you also have become dead to the law** through the body of Christ, that you may be married to another — to Him who was raised from the dead, that we should bear fruit to God. 5 For when we were in the flesh, the sinful passions which were aroused by the law were at work in our members to bear fruit to death. 6 But now **we have been delivered from the law**, having died to what we were held by, so that we should serve in the newness of the Spirit and **not in the oldness of the letter**."* (Rom 7:4-6)

Those who argue for carrying parts of the Law over into the New Covenant would usually argue that what we were freed from was only the ceremonial aspects of the Law, but we continue to be under the Ten Commandments. However, Paul in the very next verse makes it clear that by saying *"Law,"* he includes also the Ten Commandments, when he says:

"What shall we say then? Is the law sin? Certainly not! On the contrary, I would not have known sin except through the law. For I would not have known covetousness unless the law had said, 'You shall not covet." (Rom 7:7)

The only place where we find mention of the commandment, *"Thou shall not covet"* is in the Ten Commandments. He quotes the tenth commandment to demonstrate that the law's purpose was to bring us to recognize our sin. It was a tutor to lead us to Christ, but now that Christ has come and He lives in us, we are no longer under the tutor *(Gal 2:25)*. It should be obvious to all, that Paul's struggle to keep the Law, described throughout the rest of chapter seven, is not a struggle to observe the sacrificial ordinances of the Law. His struggle was with the Ten Commandments.

Another clear evidence that the Ten Commandments are included in Paul's references to the Law, which we are said to no longer be under, is found in 2Corinthians 3:

*"who also made us sufficient as ministers of the new covenant, not of the letter but of the Spirit; for the letter kills, but the Spirit gives life. 7 But if the ministry of death, **written and engraved on stones**, was glorious, so that the children of Israel could not look steadily at the face of Moses because of the glory of his countenance, which glory was passing away, 8 how will the ministry of the Spirit not be more glorious? 9 For if the ministry of condemnation had glory, the ministry of righteousness exceeds much more in glory. 10 For even what was made glorious had no glory in this respect, because of the glory that excels. 11 For if **what is passing away** was glorious, what remains is much more glorious." (2Cor 3:6-11)*

Paul says that the letter which kills is the *ministry of death* which was **written and engraved on stones**. There are over 600 laws contained in the Law of Moses, but only the ten were written by God on tablets of stone. Only the tablets containing the Ten Commandments were placed *within* the Ark of the Covenant. The other laws were written on a scroll and placed *beside* the Ark of the Covenant:

21

*"When Moses had finished writing down on a scroll every single word of this law, 25 he commanded the Levites who carried the ark of the Lord's covenant, 26 'Take this book of the law and **place it beside the ark** of the covenant of the Lord your God, so that it may remain there as a witness against you." (Deut 31:24-26 HCS)*

Some point to the King James Version's rendering of 1John 3:4: *"Whosoever committeth sin transgresseth also the law: for **sin is the transgression of the law**"* as evidence that we are still under the Law. However, *"transgression of the Law"* is an incorrect translation of the Greek *anomía*, which simply means *"lawlessness."* The word refers to *iniquity, insubordination,* or *wickedness,* and not specifically to the transgression of the Mosaic Law. Almost every other translation has corrected this error, as we see in the New King James Version which says: *"Whoever commits sin also commits lawlessness, and **sin is lawlessness**."*

Therefore, the Ten Commandments, including the weekly Sabbath, along with the rest of the commandments of the law which were a witness against us and whose requirements were contrary to us - separating us from God, were taken out of the way, having been nailed to His cross. Paul makes this very clear in his epistle to the Colossians:

*"And you, being dead in your trespasses and the uncircumcision of your flesh, He has made alive together with Him, having forgiven you all trespasses, 14 **having wiped out the handwriting of** requirements (Gr. dogma "ley, ordinance") **that was against us, which was contrary to us**. And He has taken it out of the way, having nailed it to the cross. 15 Having disarmed principalities and powers, He made a public spectacle of them, triumphing over them in it. 16 So let no one judge you in **food or in drink**, or regarding a **festival** or a **new moon** or **sabbaths**, 17 **which are a shadow** of things to come, but the substance is of Christ." (Col 2:13-18)*

The phrase, *"the handwriting of requirements that was against us,"* is referring to the entire Law of the Old Covenant. This becomes evident comparing this passage with another complementary passage in Ephesians where Paul uses the same word "requirements" (Gr. *dogma* "ley, ordinance"), clearly referring to the Old Covenant Law: *"having abolished in His flesh the enmity, that is, the law of commandments contained in **ordinances** (dogma)." (Eph*

2:15 cf. 2Cor 3:6-11). It becomes even more evident that the Law was that which was nailed to the cross, seeing the application of the declaration made by Paul beginning in verse 16.

Paul begins verse 16 saying, *"So (therefore)....,* naming several ordinances under the Law which are no longer applicable to us under the New Covenant. The most notable of these is the fourth of the Ten Commandments – the Sabbath. That the *"sabbaths"* mentioned here refer to the weekly Sabbaths, becomes clear upon examining the Old Testament instructions concerning the annual, monthly and weekly Sabbath observances. On numerous occasions we see this same order of annual, monthly and weekly observances here listed in Colossians 2:16, repeated throughout the Old Testament:

> *"and at every presentation of a burnt offering to the Lord on the* **Sabbaths** *and on the* **New Moons** *and on the* **set feasts***, by number according to the ordinance governing them, regularly before the Lord." (1Chron 23:31)*

> *"for the showbread, for the regular grain offering, for the regular burnt offering of the* **Sabbaths***, the* **New Moons***, and the* **set feasts***." (Neh 10:33, cf. Nu 28:9-31; Ezek 45:17; 46:1-11)*

The Christian Sabbath, of which the Jewish Sabbath was just a shadow, is not just one day each week. For us now, it is a continual rest from our own works which we enter into by faith in Christ, who now lives out His resurrection life in us, as we rest. *(Heb 4:9,10)* Those who believe that they are to some degree under the Law, are referred to by Paul as brethren who are weak in their new-found faith in Christ:

> *"Receive one who is* **weak in the faith***, but not to disputes over doubtful things. 2 For one believes he may eat all things, but* **he who is weak eats only vegetables***. 3 Let not him who eats despise him who does not eat, and let not him who does not eat judge him who eats; for God has received him. 4 Who are you to judge another's servant? To his own master he stands or falls. Indeed, he will be made to stand, for God is able to make him stand. 5* **One person esteems one day above another; another esteems every day alike***.* **Let each be fully convinced in his own mind***." (Rom 14:1-5)*

Don't think for one moment that Paul would simply say concerning days: *"Let each be fully convinced in his own mind"* if we, as believers under the New Covenant, were still obligated to keep the Sabbath. According to Paul, holding on to Law observance was an indication that one was weak in faith, not fully believing that we are now free from the Law and joined to Christ.

However, there are many believers who acknowledge that we are no longer under the Jewish Sabbath and that Sunday isn't the Sabbath, but rather, the first day of the Jewish week. On Sunday, the first day of the Jewish week, our Lord raised from the dead, and for that reason we come together on Sundays, as did the early Church. For these brethren, it is not the Eleven Commandments, nor the Ten Commandments. For them, what remains are the Nine Commandments – all the ten with the exception of the Sabbath. For many, it is just too difficult to grasp the truth that the entire Old Covenant system has passed away, having been replaced by the New.

Did the Old Covenant Law really pass away, making way for the New?

> *"For if what is **passing away** was glorious, what remains is much more glorious." (2Cor 3:11)*

Those who insist upon retaining certain elements of the Old Covenant point to the words of Jesus in His Sermon on the Mount when He said concerning the Law and the Prophets:

> *"Do not think that I came to destroy the Law or the Prophets. **I did not come to destroy but to fulfill**. 18 For assuredly, I say to you, till heaven and earth pass away, one jot or one tittle will by no means pass from the law **till all is fulfilled**. 19 Whoever therefore breaks one of the least of these commandments, and teaches men so, shall be called least in the kingdom of heaven; but whoever does and teaches them, he shall be called great in the kingdom of heaven. 20 For I say to you, that unless your righteousness exceeds the righteousness of the scribes and Pharisees, you will by no means enter the kingdom of heaven." (Matt 5:17-20)*

It is important to keep in mind that Jesus is here speaking under the Old Covenant. He had not yet entirely fulfilled the Old, so as to take it out of the way entirely, nailing it to His cross *(Col 2:14)*. Although the Pharisees were the strictest and most meticulous law-keeping sect in existence, they had lowered the Law's requirement of absolute perfection *(James 2:10)*. The purpose of the Law was to reveal our sinful, lost condition, leading to despair of self-salvation, but the Pharisees had reduced the requirements of the Law to a somewhat manageable, external obedience.

Jesus, beginning here in Matthew 5:17, and continuing until the end of the chapter, raises the bar higher than that of the Pharisees and even beyond the letter of the Law of Moses. He told them that if one were to break even the least of the more than 600 commandments, he would be called least in the kingdom of heaven. He then proceeded to raise the bar even more impossibly high, saying that just calling someone a fool is like breaking the sixth commandment: *"thou shall not kill."* He said that just looking at a woman in a sexual way, constitutes a breaking of the seventh commandment: *"thou shall not commit adultery."* And He continues telling them in various ways, that just fulfilling the letter of the Law wasn't enough.

Does it make you feel encouraged and motivated reading and reflecting upon Jesus' words in this passage? Does it inspire you to greater heights, or does it lead you to despair of any hope of salvation by works? Any honest person would ask: *"who then can be saved?"* Jesus' intent was not to motivate us, or bolster our self-confidence, but to bring His hearers to despair of ever achieving any righteousness of our own, in order that we would be prepared to receive His righteousness as a gift of grace after He went to the cross and established the New Covenant of Grace. He was using the Law as a tutor to lead them to Himself for salvation.

Paul, in Romans, uses the same strategy. In the first chapters, he demonstrates that all - Jew and Gentile alike, stand guilty before God. In 3:19,20 he sums up our guilty condition:

*"Now we know that **whatever the law says**, it says to those who are under the law, **that every mouth may be stopped, and all the world may become guilty before God**. 20 Therefore **by the deeds of the law no flesh will be justified in His sight, for by the law is the knowledge of sin.**" (Rom 3:19-20)*

Here Paul establishes the purpose of the law, which was to give us the knowledge of our own sin, in order that we may become guilty before God. That is the very same thing that Jesus was doing in the Sermon on the Mount, except that Paul was living on the other side of the cross, and so he was able to present to them the good news of the gospel – the solution to our dilemma, offered through the New Covenant. After showing them their hopeless condition, he announces:

*"**But now** the righteousness of God **apart from the law** is revealed, being witnessed by the Law and the Prophets, 22 **even the righteousness of God, through faith in Jesus Christ**, to all and on all who believe. For there is no difference; 23 for all have sinned and fall short of the glory of God, 24 **being justified freely by His grace** through the redemption that is in Christ Jesus."* (Rom 3:21-24)

But let us return now to the words of Jesus, in Matthew 5:17-20: *"Do not think that I came to destroy the Law or the Prophets. I did not come to destroy **but to fulfill**. For assuredly, I say to you, till heaven and earth pass away, one jot or one tittle will by no means pass from the law **till all is fulfilled**."*

Those who insist that the Ten Commandments are still in force for the believer today under the New Covenant, use this as evidence that not one jot or tittle has passed from the Law. But I would ask them, did Jesus mean to say that we are still under all of the Law, with its 600 plus commandments? All would agree that, at least the Law's sacrificial system has *passed away*, having been *fulfilled* by Jesus in His death and resurrection. Just that portion of the Law alone contained hundreds of jots and tittles (orthographic accents). Most also would concede that the other ceremonial prohibitions of the Law also passed away, including food and drink, dress, and even the Fourth Commandment, which prohibited any work being done on the Sabbath within one's household, including the animals. Also, all prophecies in the Prophets concerning Him were fulfilled, and therefore have passed away, not having any future application.

What then did Jesus intend for us to understand when He said: *"till heaven and earth pass away, one jot or one tittle will by no means pass from the law till all is fulfilled"*? The answer should be obvious. It would be easier for heaven and earth to pass away than for one word spoken by the Lord to pass away *without being fulfilled*. Every word which proceeds out of the mouth of God must be *fulfilled*. But, now let me ask another question, did Jesus come *to fulfill* the Law and the Prophets? Yes. Did He accomplish His mission? Again, the answer is a resounding yes. If He hadn't fulfilled the Law and the Prophets, we would still be under the entirety of the Law and would still be looking for the coming of the prophesied Messiah.

When Jesus spoke to the two disciples on the road to Emmaus, He rebuked them saying: *"O foolish ones, and slow of heart to believe in all that the prophets have spoken! 26 Ought not the Christ to have suffered these things and to enter into His glory?" 27 And **beginning at Moses and all the Prophets, He expounded to them in all the Scriptures the things concerning Himself**." (Luke 24:25-27)*

What was He explaining to them from Moses and the Prophets concerning Himself? We find out later, when the two returned to Jerusalem and Jesus appeared where they were gathered with the other disciples. Jesus said to the disciples:

*"These are the words which I spoke to you while I was still with you, that **all things must be fulfilled** which were written in the **Law of Moses and the Prophets and the Psalms concerning Me**. 45 And He opened their understanding, that they might comprehend the Scriptures." (Luke 24:44-45)*

Did Jesus fulfill the Law and the Prophets? Yes. Jesus did not say that not a jot or tittle would ever pass from the Law or the Prophets, but that not a jot or tittle would pass without first being fulfilled. And in His death and resurrection, all written in the Law of Moses and the Prophets concerning Him were fulfilled. He did not destroy or simply abolish the Law – He fulfilled it. By doing that, He made the entire Old Covenant obsolete:

*"In that He says, 'A new covenant,' **He has made the first obsolete**. Now what is becoming obsolete and growing old is ready to vanish away." (Heb 8:13)*

*"For if what is **passing away** was glorious, what remains is much more glorious." (2Cor 3:11)*

I believe that if Jesus were to appear to many of us today, as He did to the two disciples on the road to Emmaus, He would rebuke us in the same way: *"O foolish ones, and slow of heart to believe in all that the prophets have spoken!"* Let us not follow the same example of unbelief concerning what Christ accomplished for us in His death and resurrection, initiating the New Covenant of grace.

The New Covenant is not according to the Letter but according to the Spirit

What many opponents of the grace movement overlook is that our new relationship with God under grace is not an external legal relationship with God through rule-keeping for acceptance, but rather a personal face to face intimate relationship based upon unconditional love and acceptance rather than fear. It is a companionship in which our spirits become one and our new heart now desires what He desires. In such a relationship of acceptance, external rules are an insult to His grace in which love - not fear, becomes the motive for service.

Paul compares the Law to the old husband, who did nothing to contribute to the relationship. The old husband was perfect, but only imposed demands which we were unable to fulfill and condemned us for falling short. Under the old husband we were enslaved to fear, always aware of our inadequacies. And there was no way of getting free because we were bound to Him by law until death. But then Jesus came and bore our sins, taking the handwriting of requirements that was against us, He took it out of the way, nailing it to His cross *(Col 2:14)*.

Through our identification with Christ, we not only died to the old adamic nature, but also to the old husband - the Law. Now, we are joined to another – to Christ, who was raised from the dead, in order that, in union with Him, we may now bear fruit for God. Now, one spirit with the Lord, we serve *in the newness of the Spirit and not in the oldness of the letter.*

"Or do you not know, brethren (for I speak to those who know the law), that the law has dominion over a man as long as he lives? 2 For the woman who has a husband is bound by the law to her husband as long as he lives. But if the husband dies, she is released from the law of her husband. 3 So then if, while her husband lives, she marries another man, she will be called an adulteress; but if her husband dies, she is free from that law, so

*that she is no adulteress, though she has married another man. 4 Therefore, my brethren, **you also have become dead to the law through the body of Christ, that you may be married to another — to Him who was raised from the dead, that we should bear fruit to God.** 5 For when we were in the flesh, the sinful passions which were aroused by the law were at work in our members to bear fruit to death. 6 **But now we have been delivered from the law, having died to what we were held by, so that we should serve in the newness of the Spirit and not in the oldness of the letter.**" (Rom 7:1-6)*

Imagine for a moment that you are a woman who had been married for many years to a stern husband, named Moses Law, who was an obsessive perfectionist. He never expressed love or affection. Not once did he complement you on a job well done, but only pointed out your errors. On the day of your marriage vows, he presented you with a framed summary of what would be expected of you as his wife and he told you to put it on the kitchen wall as a reminder of your obligations. In addition to that, he gave you a leather-bound volume with a more detailed run-down of daily does and don'ts along with instructions as to what you must do to appease him in case you failed to keep one of his rules. For years, you tried in vain to live up to his expectations until one day he said that he wasn't going to put up with you any longer and sold you as a slave in the slave market.

Then, when you were in your deepest despair, a wonderful gentleman named Jesus Fulogrés, laid eyes on you and loved you. He paid an exorbitant price for your freedom, asked you to marry him, and took you to live with him as his beloved bride. He was nothing like the first husband. He always wanted to be with you, and the things that the first husband demanded of you he wanted to do together with you. However, you were so accustomed to slavishly serving your old husband all alone, that every time your new husband wished to do something with you, you always responded: *"Oh that's OK. I'll do it myself, thank you."* Since you still had the picture-framed list your first husband gave you, you dusted it off and put it back on the kitchen wall to remind you of all the things you needed to do in order to please your new husband. Imagine how hurt your new husband would feel as he watches you day after day trying to do everything according to the letter of the old husband, without him.

Many, like the woman who was freed from the old husband, Moses, carry over the same legalistic mentality into their relationship with their new husband, Jesus. Many a child of God is like Martha, who was distracted doing many things, off somewhere serving Jesus alone instead of simply sitting at His feet as Mary did *(Luke 10:38-42)*.

Jesus invites us saying: *"Come to Me, all you who labor and are heavy laden, and I will give you rest. Take My yoke upon you and learn from Me, for I am gentle and lowly in heart, and you will find rest for your souls. For My yoke is easy and My burden is light."* But we reason that He must have meant something other than the yoke of the Law. Weary and heavy laden, we continue struggling alone in order to be accepted by our performance, and continue carrying the heavy yoke that Peter said, *"neither our fathers nor we were able to bear." (Acts 15:10)*.

To now exchange our new life in union with Christ for the letter of the Law is to nullify the grace of God, according to Paul. Yet so many in the Church-world have fallen into this very error. Christ loves us and gave Himself so that He might live His own life in and through us, yet many continue seeking to make themselves acceptable through the works of the Law as if Christ wasn't in their lives at all.

> *"For through the Law **I died to the Law**, so **that I might live to God**. 20 I have been crucified with Christ; and it is no longer I who live, but **Christ lives in me**; and the life which I now live in the flesh I live by faith in the Son of God, who loved me and gave Himself up for me. 21 **I do not nullify the grace of God, for if righteousness comes through the Law, then Christ died needlessly**." (Gal 2:19-21 NAS)*

It couldn't be any clearer than Paul has made it, that we are not to look any longer to the letter of the Law for acceptance, life and godliness, but that we should now *"serve in newness of spirit and not in oldness of the letter." (Rom 7:6)*. More of us than we would like to think have been bewitched in the same way as the Galatian believers into thinking we only begin by the Spirit, and that the rest depends upon our own fleshly efforts, through the works of the Law. *(Gal 3:1-3)*. The grace of God, for many, is not a person who is now our very life. Grace, for them, is nothing more than a turbo-charger added on to their flesh-engine.

New Covenant Injunctions and Commandments

Some object by pointing out that the New Testament contains numerous commandments, reproofs and admonitions, even after Pentecost when the New Covenant fully went into effect and the Holy Spirit came to reside in us. They argue that there is no practical difference, since we still find admonitions to obey and warnings of consequences if we don't.

At first glance this may seem like a valid argument. However, in order to understand the place for these commandments, reproofs and admonitions in the New Testament, we must see that abiding in Christ is not automatic – it requires participation on our part. There are imperatives for the abiding life, in union with Christ which, if ignored, will result in us leaving the straight and narrow grace-walk and moving back into the flesh, where correction becomes necessary. A partial list of abiding imperatives are:

*"**Abide** in Me, and I in you." (John 15:4)*

*"**Abide** in My love." (John 15:9)*

*"**Walk** in the Spirit, and you shall not fulfill the lust of the flesh." (Gal 5:16)*

*"If we live in the Spirit, let us also **walk** in the Spirit." (Gal 5:25)*

*"As you therefore have received Christ Jesus the Lord, so **walk** in Him." (Col 2:6)*

*"**Grow in the grace** and knowledge of our Lord and Savior Jesus Christ." (2Peter 3:18)*

*"**Be strong in the grace** that is in Christ Jesus." (2 Tim 2:1)*

*"**Stand fast** the[1]refore **in the liberty** by which Christ has made us free, and do not be entangled again with a yoke of bondage." (Gal 5:1)*

These are all positive imperatives to remain in the place of abiding, where we bear His fruit and His righteousness is produced

---

[1]

in us. The straight and narrow is not less traveled because it is too difficult for all but the strongest and ablest to travel on. The straight and narrow is simply abiding in Christ. It is a grace walk where we simply remain in yoke with Him - keeping our eyes upon Him. As long as we *abide* in Christ and in His love - as long as we *walk* in the Spirit, *growing strong in grace, standing fast in the liberty by which Christ made us free*, all other commandments, admonitions and warnings are superfluous.

However, it is a narrow walk and we weren't born walking. We easily take our eyes off of Jesus and fall from grace back into independent self-works, or else we misuse grace, going into licentiousness. Others receive the grace of God in vain - they simply sit on it and do not walk in it *(1Cor 15:10).*

Also, although in our innermost man – our spirit, we already have the mind of Christ, our soul needs to be renewed and sanctified. Therefore, our mind, which is of the soul, must be renewed by the word of Christ:

> **"Let the word of Christ dwell in you richly** in all wisdom, **teaching** and **admonishing** one another in psalms and hymns and spiritual songs, singing with grace in your hearts to the Lord." (Col 3:16-17)

Notice the imperative *"let."* When we received Christ, we received the mind of Christ in our newborn spirit – we already have the anointing of the Spirit and know all things in our spirit, since the day we were born again *(1Cor 2:16; 1Juan 2:20).* However, in our soul, we still need to be instructed and admonished in the Word of Christ. We need to be renewed in the spirit of our mind *(Ef 4:23).* This is not automatic. We have the Holy Spirit who will teach us all things *(Juan 14:26),* but if we do not walk in the Spirit; being full of the Spirit; letting the word of Christ renew our minds, we will continue being carnal, babes in Christ.

If we were automatically spiritual all the time, walking according to the Spirit and not according to the flesh, we would automatically be fruitful unto every good work, and His righteousness would be consistently lived out in us as a natural outgrowth of our Abiding relationship. We would be able to discern all things automatically, since we would always be living according to the mind of Christ *(1Cor*

2:15,16). However, although our born again spirit is perfect, our soul and body must be conformed to His image.

Therefore, the commands, reproofs, admonitions and warnings, should not be seen as the way to live the Christian life, but rather words of orientation and correction, designed to keep us in the straight and narrow grace-walk. Even the Old Covenant Law, along with all the Scriptures, are *profitable for doctrine, for reproof, for correction, for instruction in righteousness (2 Tim 3:16).* The problem is when we take it a step further and present the Word of Christ as if it were a rule of life for believers to live out in order to be acceptable to Him, failing to see that the Word of Christ must be lived out in our lives through Him who now lives in us. Paul addresses this error when he said:

> *"Some, having strayed, have turned aside to idle talk, 7 desiring to be teachers of the law, understanding neither what they say nor the things which they affirm. 8 But we know that **the law is good if one uses it lawfully**, 9 **knowing this: that the law is not made for a righteous person**, but for the lawless and insubordinate, for the ungodly and for sinners, for the unholy and profane, for murderers of fathers and murderers of mothers, for manslayers, 10 for fornicators, for sodomites, for kidnappers, for liars, for perjurers, and if there is any other thing that is contrary to sound doctrine, 11 **according to the glorious gospel** of the blessed God which was committed to my trust." (1 Tim 1:6-11)*

The glorious gospel is the good news that in Christ we are now perfectly righteous in our born again spirits, having received the gift of His righteousness. Presently, that same perfect righteousness is being produced in us as we simply walk in the newness of the Spirit, and not in the oldness of the Letter *(Rom 7:6).* To teach the Law rightly is to make it clear that it is not for the righteous, but for the lost. And it was not for them to live by, but to die by. For everyone outside of Christ, it serves to reveal to them their need of the Savior. But for those of us who are in Christ, we are no longer under the tutor of the Law, but in a face-to-face relationship with Christ.

Are Grace Teachers Antinomians?

Opponents of the grace movement often accuse grace teachers of being antinomians, or against the Law. However, most grace teachers would heartily agree with Paul that the Law is holy, just and good *(Rom 7:12)*. Paul, after saying that we died to the old husband of the Law, and that we are now free from it, asks the question: *"What shall we say then? Is the law sin? Certainly not! On the contrary, I would not have known sin except through the law." (Rom 7:7).* As we saw in 1Timothy, Paul says that the law is good as long as you recognize that it was not made for the righteous, but in order to show the sinner his sin. He said that if it were not for the law, he would not have known he was a sinner. The majority of grace teachers see the purpose of the Law as being exactly the same as Paul saw it. Therefore, to make them out to be antinomians would be the same as making out Paul to be an antinomian. Paul, along with Stephen, were accused by the Jews of that time of being antinomians. Paul was stoned by them, and Stephen was also stoned to death under the accusation of teaching against the Law, simply for presenting Christ as the fulfillment of the Law *(Acts 6:11-14)*.

Some opponents have even gone to the extreme of accusing grace teachers of the heresy of Marcionism. Marcion lived in the second century. He put forth a form of dualism in which the God of the Old Testament was not the same God as the God of the New Testament. He excluded the Old Testament altogether and formed a theology based upon portions of Paul's writings.

In all fairness, to my knowledge, no teacher within the grace movement even comes close to teaching Marcionism. In my opinion, the cry of heresy, is too frequently used when one does not have a strong argument from the Scriptures to back up their doctrine. It gives them an unfair advantage with the unlearned, creating in them a fear of further investigating the arguments of their opponents. This unethical practice is a hang-over from the dark ages and should be replaced with solid scriptural arguments.

Chapter two
Called to Freedom

> *"For **you were called to freedom**, brethren; only do not turn your freedom into an opportunity for the flesh, but through love serve one another. 14 For the whole Law is fulfilled in one word, in the statement, 'you shall love your neighbor as yourself." (Gal 5:13-14 NASU)*

What many of God's elect children either do not realize, or have lost sight of, is that when we were called to be united to Christ we were called to freedom. For some, their present experience is anything but freedom, and words describing our New Covenant relationship with the Lord, such as *"abundant life", "rivers of living water flowing out of our innermost being," "joy unspeakable and full of glory,"* or *"rest,"* seem to mock, rather than describe their daily experience.

Legalism brings Bondage

Those who teach we are still to some degree under the Law of Moses seek to define *freedom* as being nothing more than divine enablement to keep the Law. Others say it only refers to freedom from the ceremonial aspects of the Law. However, as we saw in the previous chapter, the Law we were made free from when we were joined to Christ, includes the Ten Commandments *(Rom 7:6,7; 2Cor 3:7,8)*. Jesus warned against putting the new wine of the Spirit of grace into the old wine-skin of the Law. Paul, defending our liberty in Christ, saying in Galatians 4 and 5 that just one point of the Law, carried over into the New Covenant of grace, makes us a debtor to keep the whole Law, and causes us to fall from grace.

The opponents of the grace movement take offense when grace teachers refer to them as *"mixed grace teachers."* However, the truth is that the majority of them do attempt to mix grace with works of the Law, which Paul says is an incompatible mix:

> *"and if by grace, then it is no longer of works; otherwise grace is no longer grace. But if it is of works, it is no longer grace; otherwise work is no longer work." (Rom 11:6)*

*"For as many as are of the works of the law are under the curse; for it is written, "Cursed is everyone who does not continue **in all things** which are written in the book of the law, to do them." (Gal 3:10)*

Some insist that we are only free from the Law for justification, but not for practical sanctification. However, we have not only been justified without the works of the Law, but we are also made perfect apart from the works the Law *(Gal 3:1-3)*. To return to the works of the Law for sanctification in our daily walk, in hope of some yet future final justification, instead of by faith believing that we have already been justified, and availing ourselves of the resurrection life of Christ, is to fall from grace. That is why Paul is so emphatic in saying:

*"**Stand fast therefore in the liberty by which Christ has made us free,** and do not be entangled again with a yoke of bondage. 2 Indeed I, Paul, say to you that if you become circumcised, Christ will profit you nothing. 3 And I testify again to every man who becomes circumcised that he is a debtor to keep the whole law. 4 **You have become estranged from Christ, you who attempt to be justified by law; you have fallen from grace**." (Gal 5:1-4)*

Paul almost sounds unchristian when he confronts this perversion of the gospel of grace, saying: *"I would that they that unsettle you would even go beyond circumcision." (Gal 5:12 ASV).* Paul literally says that he wished that those who sought to bring them under Law through the initiatory ritual of circumcision, would mutilate their male organs. Paul suffered what he described as a *second labor in birth,* until he saw Christ formed in them, because the *mixed grace* teachers (excuse the expression) had entered among them, sowing the leaven of the Law, having bewitched them into thinking that, after having begun by grace, they must now be perfected by the works of the Law. The severity of Paul is justified when one considers that it is an affront to Christ who now lives in us. There is no greater sin that a believer can commit than to spurn the grace of God, trusting instead in our own works of the Law for righteousness. As Paul says: *"I do not set aside the grace of God; **for if righteousness comes through the law, then Christ died in vain**." (Gal 2:21).*

Libertinism also brings Bondage

Apart from a mixed grace "gospel," which Paul counters in Galatians, there is also the opposite error of libertinism, which is licentiousness, or a life without restraints. Paul also counters this error in no uncertain terms in the same epistle, when he says:

*"For you, brethren, have been called to liberty; only **do not use liberty as an opportunity for the flesh**, but through love serve one another. 14 For all the law is fulfilled in one word, even in this: "You shall love your neighbor as yourself.... 19 Now the works of the flesh are evident, which are: adultery, fornication, uncleanness, lewdness, 20 idolatry, sorcery, hatred, contentions, jealousies, outbursts of wrath, selfish ambitions, dissensions, heresies, 21 envy, murders, drunkenness, revelries, and the like; of which I tell **you** beforehand, just as I also told **you** in time past, that **those who practice such things will not inherit the kingdom of God**." (Gal 5:13,14;19-21)*

Also, Jude (who modestly referred to himself as "the Lord's servant," but was in reality a half-brother to Jesus), does not mince words when speaking against this other perversion of the true grace of God when he says:

*"For certain men whose condemnation was written about long ago have secretly slipped in among you. They are godless men, **who change the grace of our God into a license for immorality and deny Jesus Christ our only Sovereign and Lord**." (Jude 4 NIV)*

Both extremes - that of legalism and libertinism, are referred to as being carnal, or of the flesh in the New Testament. Both are a denial of the transforming power of Jesus Christ who lives in us and makes out Christ's death on the cross to be of no real effect. Neither the one nor the other are the straight and narrow way of grace in union with Christ in which we have been created anew in the true righteousness and holiness of Christ, and in which the Spirit, in turn, produces that same righteousness and holiness in us as we simply walk in the Spirit with our eyes upon Jesus.

Sadly however, the true grace of God is not proclaimed in its pure form from most pulpits today. What is usually presented is either law with a self-empowering version of grace, or the other extreme of a self-indulging all-permissive concept of grace, where the Father indulges His children, and would never intervene against sin in their lives. Both are self-centered and not Christ centered. Promotion of self, no matter how you dress it, is flesh. Self is just flesh spelled backwards, and is against the Spirit, no matter how you spell it.

Redefining Grace

Many opponents of the grace movement, alarmed that so many convert the grace of God into licentiousness, seek to redefine grace in such a way that it becomes nothing more than God's empowerment of self or the flesh, thus enabling us to keep the Law. I see their version of grace as being comparable to a turbo-charger, which is an accessory that can be added to a conventional piston engine, thus increasing its power. However, grace in the Scriptures is more than something to assist our old man in Adam. Grace makes us into a new creation altogether, in which our engine is no longer the old adamic self, but the very life of Christ himself in us. In this analogy, our old motor died, and through the new birth we received an entirely new and distinct engine – not a piston engine, as we were in Adam, but an entirely new turbine-jet engine. In this analogy, grace is not simply that which supplements our old nature, but that which removes the old man altogether, replacing it with the new man in Christ.

The word translated *grace* in Greek is *cháris*. There are other variations of *cháris* used in the New Testament. The word for *"spiritual gift"* is *charisma,* which *Strong's defines as "divine gratuity," charítzomai, which means "to freely or graciously give or forgive,"* and the verb *charitáo* means *"to grace or highly favor."* The underlying idea in all forms of *cháris* in the New Testament is that of *favor freely given.* In the case of us receiving the favor of God, it is always unmerited, since none of us are deserving of His favor, and therefore we normally define grace as *"unmerited favor."*

Some mixed-grace teachers, however, say that *"unmerited favor"* is an overused term, since grace often refers to empowerment to serve. While it is true that grace often refers to empowerment, it is still unmerited favor, since the empowerment doesn't originate in us, but is given to us:

*"But **by the grace of God I am what I am**, and His grace toward me was not in vain; but I labored more abundantly than they all,*

yet not I, but the grace of God which was with me." (1Cor 15:10)

Paul here makes it clear that the grace that empowered him for service was God's unmerited favor towards him. And he is careful to emphasize that all he had accomplished wasn't really him, but God's grace in him. It is significant to note that Paul uses similar phrases when referring to the life of Christ in him, as he does concerning the grace of God in him. He said:

"I have been crucified with Christ; **it is no longer I who live, but Christ lives in me;** *and the life which I now live in the flesh I live by faith in the Son of God, who loved me and gave Himself for me." (Gal 2:20)*

Grace does not simply consist of favors or empowerment – it is the very person of Christ who lives in us. If you are in Christ, you are in grace: The grace empowering you for service is nothing more or less than Christ in you. As Paul said: *"I can do all things through Christ who strengthens me." (Philippians 4:13).* One could say: *"I can do all things through grace which strengthens me"* without changing the meaning of what Paul wished to express.

Typically, the opponents of the grace message will argue that it is incorrect to say that grace is the person of Jesus. One author said that grace cannot be a person because it is a noun. However, Jesus is also called "the *way,* the *truth* and the *life.*" These are all nouns, but no Christian would deny that Jesus is the way, the truth or the life. He is also called *"the Door," "the Lamb"* and *"the Lion,"* all of which are nouns. I personally find it difficult to imagine how anyone who has come to know Jesus as their justification, redemption, sanctification, wisdom and their very life, would have difficulty accepting that Jesus himself is the personification of grace.

They point out that not every text in the New Testament, where the word *"grace"* appears, would make logical sense if the name *"Jesus"* was used in the place of *"grace."* However, the same could be said concerning other nouns used to refer to Jesus such as *"the truth,"* but no one would deny that Jesus is the truth.

Some opponents have characterized the grace presented by the grace movement as *"cheap grace."* Although it is true that some seek to convert the grace of God into licentiousness, *"cheap grace"* is an anomaly because grace is, in and of itself, *a gift,* freely given to unworthy sinners. The grace of God is by no means cheap, but it is free. The grace of God is priceless, but it is given without price. The moment someone tries to put a price-tag on grace it ceases to be grace and becomes something that must be earned by works. Paul makes this clear when he says: *"...there is a remnant according to the election of grace. And **if by grace, then it is no longer of works; otherwise grace is no longer grace**. But if it is of works, it is no longer grace; otherwise work is no longer work." (Rom 11:5b,6).* Receiving and walking in the grace of God inevitably results in works, just as receiving and abiding in Christ bears fruit, but we must *freely* receive both.

We must hold fast to our freedom in the true grace of God, with our eyes stayed upon Jesus, the author and finisher of faith. Too many react against legalism and end up in libertinism, or move into legalism as a reaction against libertinism. True grace and freedom come from abiding in Christ, allowing His life and works to be lived out through us.

The grace revolution has introduced many a weary, heavy laden believer into His rest in which the Christian life is lived out *through them* by the Spirit of Christ, *by grace,* rather than *by them.* However, there are also certain doctrines prevalent within the movement which, if not corrected, could derail the grace movement, going beyond the doctrine of Christ into licentiousness. Many of these same grace teachers express their disappointment and consternation as they see so many under their own teachings that seem to have missed the message of the true grace of God and are using grace as a green light to continue on in a life of sin.

Admonitions against Licentiousness

What I perceive as harmful errors within the grace movement will be considered at a later time. However, in spite of the errors and excesses we may see within the movement, we must avoid being reactionary, moving into a form of legalism in order to avoid libertinism. We must *stand fast in the liberty by which Christ has made us free, and not be entangled again with a yoke of bondage,* either by embracing a mixed grace message or continuing in sin in the name of grace.

A major part of learning to walk in the liberty we have in Christ is to know how to exercise our liberty in a loving, non-destructive way. Paul said concerning our liberty:

"All things are lawful for me, but all things are not helpful. All things are lawful for me, but I will not be brought under the power of any." (1Cor 6:12)

"All things are lawful for me, but not all things are helpful; all things are lawful for me, but not all things edify. Let no one seek his own, but each one the other's well-being." (1Cor 10:23)

The believers in Corinth differed from those in Galatia in that they knew that they were free from the Law. Yet they were using their liberty as an occasion for the flesh, instead of serving one another in love *(Gal 5:13)*. As a result, they were carnal, indulging their own fleshly desires in the name of grace and Christian liberty. When they came together it wasn't for edification. They used the gifts of the Spirit with selfish motives and not for edification. They even abused the Lord's Supper, with some gorging themselves and getting drunk on the wine, while others went hungry *(1Cor 11:20,21)*.

Paul, however, did not do what many leaders often do with those who abuse grace. He did not try to put them under law or redefine grace. Instead he reminded them of who they were, calling them saints, and reminding those who were practicing idolatry and fornication that their bodies were members of Christ and that they were one spirit with Him. He reminded them that they had been bought with a price, and that their bodies were the temple of the Holy Spirit *(1Cor 1:2; 6:15-19)*.

He did, however, do what many grace teachers fail to do: *he admonished them,* telling them that they needed to examine themselves to make sure that Christ was really in them, since the conduct of many among them gave no evidence that Christ was truly in them *(2Cor 13:5)*. Then *he warned them* against being deceived into thinking that those who do not bear fruit corresponding to our new life in Christ will, nevertheless, inherit the kingdom of heaven:

*"Do you not know that **the unrighteous will not inherit the kingdom of God? Do not be deceived.** Neither fornicators, nor idolaters, nor adulterers, nor homosexuals, nor sodomites, 10 nor thieves, nor covetous, nor drunkards, nor revilers, nor extortioners*

*will inherit the kingdom of God. 11 **And such were some of you.
But you were washed, but you were sanctified, but you were
justified in the name of the Lord Jesus and by the Spirit of
our God.**" (1Cor 6:9-11)*

Grace teachers generally either disarm or ignore entirely most of
the stern admonitions and warnings found in the New Testament.
Paul's obvious intention here was to expose the deception that would
lead any among them into thinking that they had been cleansed,
sanctified and justified when there was no outward indication of it in
their lives.

However, some grace teachers make this admonition out to say
just the opposite. They say that, what Paul really meant to say was
that - because one's identity has changed, even when one practices
these sins, nothing can change who he now is in Christ. Whereas
Paul was saying: "Don't be deceived into thinking you have been
born again if you are still practicing sin," they make him out to be
saying that, because you have been born again, even though you
are still living in sin, you are now righteous in God's eyes and
acceptable to Him. Although that might be true in the case of some
new and immature believers who are nevertheless born again, in the
context Paul wanted those persisting in a lifestyle of sin to consider
the possibility that they may not have truly believed unto salvation.

The apostle John does the same in 1John when he says: *"Little
children, let no one deceive you. He who practices righteousness is
righteous, just as He is righteous." (1John 3:7)*. They are both saying
that the proof of the new birth is in the fruit. However, some grace
teachers present the admonition as though Paul was affirming them
in their sins.

This tendency towards affirming those yet practicing sin, has in
turn led to a disregard for Paul's instructions concerning how to deal
with sin within the Church. The disciplinary measure he commanded
the Corinthians to take concerning the brother living in fornication
with his father's wife: *"deliver such a one to Satan for the destruction
of the flesh, that his spirit may be saved in the day of the Lord Jesus"
(1Cor 5:5)*, would be considered unloving and unacceptable by many
within the grace movement. However, in his second epistle, we see
that Paul's severe disciplinary measure led both to the Corinthians
repenting of boasting in their tolerance of sin, and also to the
restoration of the sinning brother *(2Cor 2:6-11; 7:8-12)*.

In 1Corinthians five, after commanding them to take disciplinary action concerning the brother in fornication, he then reproaches them for boasting of their tolerance of sin among them: *"Your glorying is not good. Do you not know that a little leaven leavens the whole lump?" (1Cor 5:6).* Some within the grace movement today do exactly what Paul says we should not do – they boast in their tolerance of sin within the Church. One prominent grace teacher actually said that he would rather share the Lord's Supper with a gay pastor than with a legalist pastor. Such glorying is not good, according to Paul.

Priding oneself in their tolerance of persistent sin among so called brethren would not have been tolerated by Paul. In continuation, he says that we are to separate ourselves from sinners who call themselves believers - however not from the sinners in the world. Our Lord Jesus himself was a friend of sinners. But when it comes to sin in the lives of those who profess to be brothers in the Lord, that is a different matter. He says:

"I wrote to you in my epistle not to keep company with sexually immoral people. 10 Yet I certainly did not mean with the sexually immoral people of this world, or with the covetous, or extortioners, or idolaters, since then you would need to go out of the world. 11 But now I have written to you not to keep company with anyone named a brother, who is sexually immoral, or covetous, or an idolater, or a reviler, or a drunkard, or an extortioner — not even to eat with such a person." (1Cor 5:9-11)

This insistence upon godly living is sound doctrine according to Paul *(1Tim 1:10).* And he warns that *"the time will come when they will not endure sound doctrine; but after their own lusts shall they heap to themselves teachers, having itching ears; and they shall turn away their ears from the truth, and shall be turned unto fables." (2Tim 4:3,4 KJV).*

If you are under a grace teaching that is intolerant of such sound doctrine, as Paul defines it, and you also find yourself becoming intolerant of such admonitions, beware, or you may find yourself becoming part of the fulfillment of this prophecy, spoken through Paul, concerning the last days.

However, if one finds himself in danger of departing from sound doctrine the answer is not to pass over into the false security of legalism but rather to put their eyes upon Jesus and look to Him as their source of life and true godliness. It is the grace of God and not the Law which teaches us that *"denying ungodliness and worldly lusts, we should live soberly, righteously, and godly in the present age." (Titus 2:12).*

Christ has truly made us free – not only free from the Law, but also free from sin *(Rom 6:7,22),* from condemnation *(Rom 8:1),* from the power of Satan, from the fear of death *(Heb 2:14,15),* and from sin consciousness *(Heb 9:14).* But we must *stand fast in the liberty by which Christ has made us free.*

Those who walk in Freedom will Suffer Persecution

*"Tell me, you who desire to be under the law, do you not hear the law? For it is written that Abraham had two sons: the one by a bondwoman, the other by a freewoman. But he who was of the bondwoman was born **according to the flesh**, and he of the freewoman **through promise**, which things are symbolic. For **these are the two covenants: the one from Mount Sinai which gives birth to bondage, which is Hagar — for this Hagar is Mount Sinai in Arabia, and corresponds to Jerusalem which now is, and is in bondage with her children — but the Jerusalem above is free, which is the mother of us all...***
*Now we, brethren, as Isaac was, are children of promise. But, **as he who was born according to the flesh then persecuted him who was born according to the Spirit, even so it is now**. Nevertheless, what does the Scripture say? 'Cast out the bondwoman and her son, for the son of the bondwoman shall not be heir with the son of the freewoman.' So then, brethren, we are not children of the bondwoman but of the free.' Stand fast therefore in the liberty by which Christ has made us free, and do not be entangled again with a yoke of bondage." (Gal 4:21-26, 28-5:1)*

Just as Ishmael's seed has always opposed Isaac's seed, Israel, so also those who are of the flesh will always oppose those who are of the promise. Those who are of the flesh will always be opposed to those who are of the Spirit. No matter what form the flesh takes, whether it be self-righteous, legalistic flesh, or self-indulging promiscuous flesh, they are both of the world, and the flesh rises up against those who simply walk in the Spirit, and freely and undeservedly receive the Father's favor. As the elder son despised seeing his prodigal brother lavished with the father's unconditional acceptance and blessings, so also those who labor for the Father's acceptance despise those who, by grace, obtain freely the promises. Those who are still encamped around Mount Sinai cannot endure seeing the sons of promise already seated with Christ in the heavenly Jerusalem.

Throughout the history of the Church the greatest persecutor of the children of promise has not been the secular world but the institutional church which moved away from the true grace of God upon entering into the Dark Ages. The institutionalized church suppressed all truth concerning the grace of God for acceptance and transformation, replacing it with a complex system of works, based upon the Ten Commandments, with their own prescribed penances for every infraction. Dante's version of hell was graphically presented to them in literature, theatres, paintings and religious architecture in order to keep the people under subjection and enslaved to a continual bondage to fear. The Bible, which contained the gospel of grace that could set them free, was kept from the public. The few who discovered the grace of God were often condemned, tortured and killed as heretics. With the printing and distribution of the Bible came the rediscovery of justification by faith alone, apart from the works of the Law. But thousands of believers were martyred at the hands of the Roman Catholic Church, during the Reformation, for insisting that salvation is not by works but by the grace of God.

Therefore, we must stand fast *in the liberty by which Christ has made us free,* not allowing ourselves to *be entangled again with a yoke of bondage,* having *our hearts established by grace,* and *not moved away from the hope of the gospel which we have heard (Gal 5:1; Heb 13:9; Col 1:23).*

Chapter three
What's New about Us?

"Therefore, if anyone is in Christ, he is a new creation; old things have passed away; behold, all things have become new." (2Cor 5:17)

The above text is an all-time favorite which is often cited but little understood by most Christians. We know that a change took place when we received Christ, but it usually doesn't take much time to realize that there is much about us that doesn't appear to be new. When we look in the mirror, we see the same gray hair and wrinkles we had before salvation. Also, it doesn't take long to realize that our personality traits tend to continue as before. If we were mentally challenged before coming to Christ, we continue being mentally challenged after receiving Him. If we were short tempered, timid, outspoken or insecure before, those traits continue to challenge us to some degree, no matter how much we may confess that we are a new creation in Christ.

Part of the problem with our understanding of this verse is that the translations of the text most of us know by memory are erroneous and misleading. The words *"things"* and *"all things"* are not in the original Greek text but were added by the translators. Actually, the English word "thing/s" doesn't even have an equivalent in the Greek language, and when the translators supply the word "things," it often changes the meaning intended by the authors. Also *"have passed away"* and *"have become"* are singular verbs, rather than plural, and should have been translated *"has passed away"* and *"has come."*

This translation error is, at least in part, due to their failure to see the distinction between the soul and the spirit. To them, if anything about us is new, it is the entire inner man – including the spirit/soul. But, in reality, the soul is distinct from the spirit, and it is only the spirit which has been created anew. Some translations have corrected these errors, as we see in *the English Standard Version: "Therefore, if anyone is in Christ, he is a new creation. **The old has passed away**; behold, **the new has come.**" (2Co 5:17 ESV)*

There is a world of difference between saying: *"old **things** have passed away and **all things** have become new,* and saying: *"**The**

47

old has passed away and the new has come." The popular translations make it seem to be saying that *everything* about us passed away and *everything* about us is now new. However, taking this verse together with the one which precedes it, we see that Paul doesn't include our physical bodies as being part of the new which has already come:

> *"Therefore, from now on, we regard no one **according to the flesh**. Even though we have known Christ **according to the flesh**, yet now we know Him thus no longer. 17 Therefore, if anyone is in Christ, he is a new creation; old things have passed away; behold, all things have become new." (2Cor 5:16-17)*

What Paul is saying is that we should no longer see and know one another according to the old physical part of us – the flesh, but rather we should learn to see and know one another according to the new spirit-man that we now are in Christ. I believe I could safely say that no one would insist that we received a new physical body the moment we believed. Until this corruptible puts on incorruption and this mortality puts on immortality, the new man within us is still contained in earthen vessels *(1Cor 15:53,54; 4:7)*. Our physical perception through the five senses of sight, smell, taste, touch and hearing, haven't changed. Our emotional makeup and minds are being renewed, but they didn't immediately become new the moment we received Christ. Therefore, it is incorrect to say that in Christ *all things* concerning us are now already new. What then is new about us? The answer is clearly set forth in the New Testament.

Body Soul and Spirit

> *"Now may the God of peace Himself sanctify you **completely**; and may your whole **spirit, soul,** and **body** be preserved blameless at the coming of our Lord Jesus Christ. 24 He who calls you is faithful, who also will do it." (1Thess 5:23-24)*

In order to comprehend what has already taken place in our new creation, we must understand the makeup of the entire man, according to the Scriptures. Man is seen in the above text to be made up of *body, soul* and *spirit*.

The natural man, outside of Christ, has only been aware of two components – our body and our soul. The Greek word for soul is *psuque*. From this word we derive the word *"psychology,"* which is the study of the soul. Most do not even recognize the existence of the innermost, immaterial part of man – his spirit. Even in the older post Reformation theological works, soul and spirit are not distinguished. Strong's concordance, printed in 1890, defines the human spirit as *"the rational soul."* However, although the natural man and even the theologians coming out of the Dark Ages, saw no distinction between soul and spirit, the Scriptures reveal a clear-cut distinction between the two:

> *"For the word of God is living and powerful, and sharper than any two-edged sword, piercing even to the division of soul and spirit, and of joints and marrow, and is a discerner of the thoughts and intents of the heart." (Heb 4:12)*

The living Word of God is able to distinguish what human wisdom and understanding cannot discern – it reveals when we are living according to our soul, being *soulish*, or living according to our spirit, being *spiritual*. Although the older translations have done much to obscure this important distinction between our soul and spirit, the original text of the New Testament clearly distinguishes between those who live according to their soul, calling them *"soulish"* and those living according to their spirit, calling them *"spiritual."* Paul, in 1Corinthians 2, contrasts the *"soulish"* man, who is governed by his soul (by what he thinks and feels in the natural), from the man who lives according to his spirit, or the *"spiritual"* man:

> *"These things we also speak, not in words which man's wisdom teaches but which the Holy Spirit teaches, comparing spiritual things with spiritual. 14 But the natural (psuquikos – "soulish") man does not receive the things of the Spirit of God, for they are foolishness to him; nor can he know them, because they are spiritually discerned. 15 But he who is spiritual judges all things, yet he himself is rightly judged by no one." (1Cor 2:13-15)*

Here we see that the word translated *"natural"* is *psuquikos,* or that which pertains to the soul *(psuque),* and literally means *"soulish"* as opposed to *pneumatikos* or *"spiritual."* But here they rendered *psuquikos* as *"natural,"* thereby diminishing the Scripture's ability to distinguish between soul and spirit. Again, we see that James, in James 3:15, contrasts the wisdom from above, which is spiritual, with earthly wisdom, which is *"soulish."* But here they translated *psuquikos* as *"sensual"* in the King James Version, instead of *"soulish,"* again blurring the distinction between soul and spirit. In

49

Jude, warning is given against *"soulish"* men who *have not a spirit,* that turn the grace of God into licentiousness *(Jude 19),* but once again it is translated *"sensual"* in most translations. [2]

Also, in 1Corinthians 15:44-46, a contrast is made between our *soulish (psuquikos) bodies,* and our *spiritual bodies,* which we will receive at Christ's Second Coming. Paul's intention was to make a contrast between our mortal body, which is *"soulish,"* or influenced by our natural emotions, intellect and will, and the incorruptible *spiritual* bodies, which we will receive in the resurrection. But again, it is translated *"natural"* by most translations. The only version I could find, which literally translated the word *psuquikos* as *"soulish"* consistently throughout the entire New Testament, was the Concordant Literal Version. It is true that *"natural"* and *"sensual"* are terms descriptive of a soulish person, who lives according to his senses, being influenced by what he sees in the natural, rather than being spiritually minded. However, both renderings fail to maintain the clear-cut distinction between the spirit and soul, as the Word of God does, when rightly translated, as Hebrews 4:12 declares.

Only our Spirit has been recreated

What many Christians do not understand is that when Paul said in 2Corinthians 5:17 that in Christ we are now a new creation, he was referring to the new birth of our spirit, and not our entire being. Jesus made it clear to Nicodemus in John 3 that it is our spirit which is born again:

"Jesus answered and said to him, 'Most assuredly, I say to you, **unless one is born again, he cannot see the kingdom of God.'** *4 Nicodemus said to Him, 'How can a man be born when he is*

---

[2] Although most translations translate the phrase *"do not have the spirit"* as referring to the Holy Spirit, the word spirit is anarthrous (without the definite article), and is probably saying that they do not have a born again spirit. That reading also maintains the contrast between the soul and the spirit of man in the context. This is also the understanding of the Greek scholar Kenneth Wuest in his Expanded New Testament where he translates it: *"These are those individuals who cause divisions, egocentric,* **not holding the spirit [the human spirit,** *that is, being egocentric, they ignore their human spirit which has to do with the spiritual, religious part of a person's life].*" (from The New Testament: An Expanded Translation by Kenneth S. Wuest Copyright © 1961 by Wm. B. Eerdmans Publishing Co.)

*old? Can he enter a second time into his mother's womb and be born?' 5 Jesus answered, 'Most assuredly, I say to you, unless one is born of water and the Spirit, he cannot enter the kingdom of God. 6 That which is born of the flesh is flesh, and **that which is born of the Spirit is spirit**. 7 Do not marvel that I said to you, 'You must be born again.' 8 The wind blows where it wishes, and you hear the sound of it, but cannot tell where it comes from and where it goes. So is everyone who is born of the Spirit." (John 3:3-8)*

Jesus reproached Nicodemus for being a teacher in Israel, yet not understanding the new birth. We find it amusing when he asked Jesus how a man could possibly enter a second time into his mother's womb and be born again. Yet many of us are just as confused as to what part of us was born again in the new creation. Jesus explained to him that even as we had to be physically born of water (referring to the breaking of the amniotic water, necessary for physical birth), even so our spirit must be born of the Holy Spirit. He makes this even clearer in the following verse when he says: *"That which is born of the flesh is flesh, and **that which is born of the Spirit is spirit**."*

It is the spirit of Adam that died the moment he partook of the fruit, not his body or his soul. When we were dead in our trespasses and sins, God made us alive in our spirit, not in our body or our soul *(Eph 2:1,5)*. Our souls were lost, but they were never dead. If our souls were to die, we would cease to exist as individuals. Our souls give us *self-consciousness*. We never lost that. Our body, with its five senses, gives us *consciousness of the material world* around us. In like manner it is our spirit which gives us *consciousness of God* and the *spiritual world*. Our spirit is that part of us which was dead unto God but was made alive in the new creation.

However, our spirit was not simply made alive - It was made alive with the very life of Christ. He is now our life *(Col 3:4)*. The eternal life which we now possess is not simply *something* we receive at the new birth. It is *someone* we receive. It is the very life of Christ as our life *(1John 5:11-13)*. We do not simply have a new spirit that can fellowship with Christ. Our spirit is one spirit with Jesus Christ: *"But he who is joined to the Lord is one spirit with Him." (1Cor 6:17)*.

Some theologians speak of our being *"in Christ"* as "positional truth," as opposed to "actual, experiential truth." They would say that

God sees us as being *positionally* in Christ but not *literally* united with Him in a *real, experiential* way. Therefore, they say that the Father sees us as being already righteous and holy *as if* we were Christ Himself, even though we are not yet righteous and holy. However, in our new man – our regenerated spirit, created anew in Christ, we were literally created perfect in true righteousness and holiness:

> *"that you put on the **new man** which **was created** according to God, in **true** righteousness and holiness." (Eph 4:24)*

The part of us that was regenerated – our spirit, was *created* in *true* (not positional) and perfect righteousness and holiness. Our brand-new spirit was born perfect in Christ – not merely "positionally," but *really* and *truly*. [3] Once we understand this reality, that we are really and truly one spirit with the Lord, many Scriptural declarations become clear. When it says that we were raised with Christ and are now seated with Him in heavenly places, we realize that it is not simply "make believe," but since our spirit is now one spirit with the Lord, we are *actually* seated with Christ in heavenly places, above all created beings, and we are already reigning in life *(Eph 2:1,6)*. Every believer already possesses the very mind of Christ and knows all things in his perfect spirit *(1Cor 2:15,16; 1John 2:20)*. While it is true that only those who are spiritual, walking according to their spirit and not according to their flesh or their soul, are able to draw from His mind, we really do already know all things in our renewed spirit. We are already exactly like Him in our new spirit man. That is what John says:

> *"Love has been perfected among us in this: that we may have boldness in the day of judgment; because **as He is, so are we in this world." (1John 4:17)***

Notice that this verse doesn't say: "Love *is being* perfected *by us*" but rather "Love **has been** perfected *among us*." It appears in perfect tense, passive voice, indicating that it has been perfected **in us**, not *by us,* in the past, resulting in us now having boldness in the Day of Judgment. Why? Because as He is, so *are we* right now, even

---

[3] While no proponent of positional truth would say that our position in Christ is not "real," for all practical purposes it is unreal because it is seen as removed from the experiential reality of who we now are in Christ through the new birth.

though we are still in this world. It doesn't simply say that we are *becoming* like Him, or that we *should be* like Him, but that **we are** as He is, right now.

No honest believer would presume to say that in their daily walk they are exactly like Jesus and that, for that reason, they have no fear of judgment. Apart from being self-deluded, such an individual would be trusting in his own merits to be accepted in the Day of Judgment and not the merits of Christ. Instead of believing that he is accepted in the Beloved, he would be ignoring the righteousness of God, given as a gift, and would be going about to establish his own righteousness *(Eph 1:6; Rom 3:21-24; 10:3,4).*

Many continue to see themselves according to the flesh and not according to the spirit. While it is true that man in Adam, outside of Christ, is referred to as "flesh" *(Gen 6:3),* as Paul says, we are no longer in the flesh but in the spirit:

> *"But you are not in the flesh; you are in the Spirit (or "spirit"), since the Spirit of God dwells in you. Anyone who does not have the Spirit of Christ does not belong to him. 10 But if Christ is in you, though the body is dead because of sin, the Spirit (spirit) is life because of righteousness." (Rom 8:9,10 NRSV)*

In many contexts where the word *"spirit"* occurs, it is uncertain whether it is our re-born spirit, or the Holy Spirit, that is being referred to, since the Greek doesn't distinguish with capitalizations. In this passage it is best to understand the first and last occurrence of *"spirit"* as referring to our human spirit. We, as born again believers, are no longer in the flesh but in the spirit. The New Revised Standard Version cited above also includes that reading in their footnote for the first and last occurrence of spirit in this passage. The new life we possess is the very life of Christ: We have become one spirit with Him. Therefore, if anyone does not have the Spirit of Christ, he does not belong to Him – he has not been born again of the Spirit and is still in the flesh. And if Christ is in us, our spirit is alive because of His righteousness.

We as believers need a revelation of who we now are in Christ. Flesh is no longer our essential nature, as it was in Adam. In Christ, our essential nature has changed. Our flesh nature was crucified with Christ and we were raised up into newness of life in Him. Our new man was created in true righteousness and holiness. We are no longer flesh but a new spirit living in a flesh-suit. I always used to think that when Paul said that God was pleased to reveal His Son in Paul *(Gal 1:15,16)*, that it was an experience unique to him. In a sense Paul's revelation of *"Christ in him"* may have been unique, but we all as believers need the same revelation of *Christ in us, the hope of glory*. We can have the words committed to memory but unless the Father reveals to us through the Spirit who we are in Christ, they are just words, and they won't make literal sense to us.

A Personal Testimony

In the year 1982, thirteen years after my initial salvation in November of 1969, I had what I can only describe as an "open heavens experience" that lasted about three months. It was similar to my initial experience of salvation when I was surprised by the baptism of the Holy Spirit in a Free-will Baptist Church in Richmond, California. I had no idea that there was such a glorious experience, and that church didn't even believe in the baptism of the Holy Spirit. That initial experience was comparable to barrels and barrels of liquid love being poured out on me and flowing from within me. During the first years of my Christian walk, I continued to live in the afterglow of that initial experience. The presence of Christ was so tangible during that time that the sinful habits I could not get free from prior to salvation, no longer had any attraction for me.

However, a few years after I was saved, I experienced a series of devastating trials. At first, I anticipated that the Lord would take the trials away, but they only increased, and He seemed to turn a deaf ear to my cries. Little by little, I lost that sensitivity to the presence of the Lord in my life. Although I didn't go back completely into my old way of life, I no longer felt that same freedom which I had formerly experienced in intimate communion with the Lord. I began to suffer anxiety attacks so constant and severe that I couldn't sleep for more than a few moments at a time for several months. I actually reached the point where I decided to take my life. I was alone with my two-year-old daughter, Kerry, in the heart of Mississippi, where hardly anybody knew me or even wanted to know a "Yankee" like me with my northern accent and long hair.

I took my daughter to the home of a Christian couple who I felt would care for her and returned to my house, where I piped the gas from the water heater into my daughter's bedroom because it was the smallest room near the water heater. When I was about to lose

54

consciousness, I had a lucid moment. I could see my daughter's little dresses hanging in the closet and realized at that moment that I couldn't leave my little two-year-old daughter without a father.

With a new determination, I turned off the gas and went to pick up my daughter. Although the depression continued, the Lord miraculously delivered me from the worst of the trials I was going through and with a new but reserved hope I returned with my daughter to California. I began looking for a Church in my area and someone recommended a church to me that was vibrant, with a lot of young people like me, which was strong in the Word. During the seven years I attended that Independent Bible Church, I dedicated myself to studying the Scriptures. I enrolled in their Bible institute and studied theology and the Greek language of the New Testament.

Although I was connected with a good church and growing in my knowledge of Scripture, I longed for that intimacy and freedom which I experienced in the beginning of my walk with the Lord. I thought that Bible knowledge would help me recapture that initial experience, but more knowledge is not a good substitute for experiencing Christ. Although the institute warned against "Bibliolatry," which amounts to worshipping the Bible instead of the God of the Bible, the cessation theology which they taught inadvertently replaced the personal relationship I once enjoyed with God for the Bible in my daily walk.

Cessationists believe that the completed Bible is what Paul referred to by *"that which is perfect"* in 1Corinthians 13:9,10 where he says: *"For we know in part and we prophesy in part." But when that which is perfect has come, then that which is in part will be done away."* They argue from this passage that the supernatural gifts such as words of knowledge and prophecy, along with all other "sign gifts," passed away when *"the perfect"* came which, according to them, is the completed Bible. However, that *"that which is perfect"* is not referring to the Bible is evident, because, in continuation, Paul says in verse 12 that when the perfect comes then we shall *"know just as we are known."* This is obviously referring to the perfect state when we are in glory and God shall be all in all, rather than to the completion of the Bible *(1Cor 15:28)*. The completion of the New Testament still leaves us seeing and knowing in part, rather than knowing even as we are known.

Cessationism inadvertently leads to a form of Bibliolatry in which we look to the Bible for direction, rather than God himself. Many

Cessationists do not even believe that we can hear the voice of God for personal guidance. God talked face to face with Abraham as a man speaks to his friend but Cessationism takes that away from us, and face to face intimacy was what I was needing and longed to recapture.

I came to a crisis three years after leaving the Bible church to live in Mendocino, California. There, an elderly pastor asked me if I would be willing to take his pastorate when he retired. I accepted and decided to study one more year of theology in San Francisco Baptist Seminary in preparation for the pastorate. After a year of intensive study in the seminary, where the staff prided themselves in being called "fighting fundamentalists" or "secondary separationists," [4] the retiring pastor, fearing that my intolerant doctrine would empty out the church, decided against retiring.

At any rate, I was in no condition to be pastoring. I was desperate and tired of trying to maintain a form of godliness without the dynamic relationship with the Lord that I had when I first believed. I went into debt to study that year in seminary, and since there wasn't any good paying work in Mendocino, I decided to work in the Bay Area where I could make good money with my secular profession. During that time, I lived in a small camper alone, and there I determined to set aside all other studies and seek to get back to where I first began in the Lord. I longed for that intimate communion with Him, but now my theology was in the way.

The first truth I rediscovered is that God still speaks to us today. Because of the Cessation doctrine and a fear of being deceived by other voices, I reached the point where I no longer heard His voice, yet I longed for that face to face relationship I had in the beginning. From the Scriptures, I began to see once again that God still speaks, but I just needed to open my ears to listen to what the Spirit was saying. Reading biographies of great evangelists and missionaries, I saw how central to their fruitfulness was their ability to hear the Lord's leading. Also, intimacy in any relationship is impossible without communication on a personal level, and I was longing to

---

[4] The belief that one must not only separate from those who do not teach sound doctrine but that we must also separate ourselves from those who do not separate themselves from those who do not teach sound doctrine.

return to that first love, when His voice used to make my heart leap for joy.

I set out to discover the secret of victory over temptation in the Christian life. For years I had struggled to no avail. I could not understand why no formula seemed to work for me. I heard a renowned conference speaker say that the secret to victory over temptation was to memorize Romans 6 thru 8 and to meditate upon it, daily reckoning oneself to be "positionally" dead with Christ to sin and alive unto God in Christ. With great expectations, I memorized all three chapters, and daily reckoned myself to be "positionally" dead to sin and alive to God in Christ Jesus. But the more I reckoned the more powerful sin's grip seemed to be. It only served to make me more sin conscious.

Then one night about ten in the evening, I was laying in the camper bed reading the book, *Abiding in Christ* by Andrew Murray, when suddenly the veil was removed from my eyes and I saw the reality of Christ as my very life. I saw that I had *indeed* died with Christ to sin and had *indeed* been raised to new life in Him. I had been taught to reckon myself *positionally* dead to sin and alive in Christ when, all along, the verse I had memorized said:

*"Likewise you also, reckon yourselves to be dead **indeed** to sin, but alive to God in Christ Jesus our Lord." (Rom 6:11)*

In a moments time, I realized that I had **indeed** died with Christ to sin and had **really** been made alive in my born again spirit. I saw that my union with Christ was *"real truth,"* and not simply *"positional truth."* In that very moment, I knew that the Father didn't simply see me as being in Christ, but that I was *indeed* in Christ and He was really in me. I saw that He didn't simply give us eternal life – He is our life *(Col 3:4)*. I now knew that the Father doesn't simply see us *as if* we were righteous in Christ, but that He *is* our righteousness. Our born again spirits have been created anew in His *true righteousness and holiness (Eph 4:24)*.

For the next three months I was in the spirit in a way that I had never dreamed possible. I felt in touch with the mind of Christ as never before. The Father was revealing His Son in me as my righteousness, my sanctification, my wisdom, my faith, and as my very life itself. The moment the veil was removed from my eyes, I could not contain my joy and ecstasy. As I received revelation upon revelation, I would break out in tears and laughter with shouts of joy unspeakable and full of glory. I remember the daily commutes, stuck in traffic, so overwhelmed with joy that everyone looked at me as if I had lost it, but I couldn't contain myself. As it was in the beginning of my walk with the Lord, temptations and the things of this world had no attraction to me whatsoever during this time.

However, as time passed, I began to feel a certain frustration because I wanted everyone around me to experience Him as I was experiencing Him. I soon realized that It was impossible to express with mere words what I was seeing and experiencing. When I tried to put into words the spiritual reality I was living, most just gave me a puzzled look, and others even reacted with frustration and resentment because they were not able to enter into the same experience.

I remember, as if it were today, after three months of experiencing the open heavens, while I was on my way home in the traffic, I said to the Lord: *"Lord, I don't want to be the only one that is experiencing you in this way. I want to be able to make you known, the way I am now knowing you."* In response, the Lord revealed to me many things in my character and understanding that needed to be changed in order to be able to make Him known. At the same time, I saw that only He could make the necessary changes. Afterwards I couldn't even remember the things He showed me that needed to be changed, but at the moment it was all very clear to me.

Then he spoke to me the words of Jesus: *"Truly, truly, I say to you, unless a grain of wheat falls into the earth and dies, it remains alone; but if it dies, it bears much fruit."* I actually remember Him asking me to choose whether I wanted to continue experiencing Him alone, as I was doing, or to allow Him to take me into death, as a grain of wheat, stripping away that outer shell of the flesh that kept His life contained within me. He said that if I would give my consent, He would take me through the painful process of death to the outer man, in order that the life of Jesus may be manifested through me. I clearly understood at that time that the kingdom of God does not consist of our limited words, but the very life of Jesus lived in and through us.

During those three months, I never audibly heard God speak to me, but His communication was much clearer than mere words. When He spoke, it was like I heard and saw what He was saying at the same time. It gave me a greater comprehension of Jesus' words when He said: *"I only do what I **see** the Father doing."* In the spirit, we not only *hear* the mind of Christ, but we **see** His mind.

When He gave me the choice to continue as I was, or allow Him to take me through death that I might bear fruit afterwards, I could not only hear what He was saying, but I could see what He was saying, and even felt His heart motive in what He planned to do. Hearing Him that way makes you want what He wants.

The last thing I remember was asking Him to promise that He would not give up on me in the process, and He said to me: "I will never leave you nor forsake you." It seemed like a foolish petition to make, being in the very presence of Love and Faithfulness Himself, but I believe He prompted me to make that request so I could hear Him personally speak this promise to me. In all the years that have followed, those have been the most important words He spoke to me during that time. That promise has been an anchor for my soul – a refuge of hope when I have felt despair of ever being a useful vessel to Him.

God didn't immediately remove His manifest presence from me. For the next couple of weeks after that conversation with Him, the sense of His presence and the revelations gradually diminished. I believe I would have literally died if He had withdrawn the sense of His presence from me immediately. As it was, I almost went insane with desire for the experience of His presence to return. I was a very dependable employee, but I almost lost my job because I would become overwhelmed with desire for His manifest presence, and out of desperation I would leave my worksite in the middle of the day, without giving notice, to seek the Lord in private with tears and loud cries.

I remember one morning at work crying out to God and saying: *"I want to see as I saw in Your presence."* Until that encounter, because of my studies, I thought I already knew most of what there was to know about God and the Christian life, but after that encounter I realized that what little I thought I knew was really nothing. I now realized that in Christ were *hidden all the treasures of wisdom and knowledge (Col 2:3).* After knowing experientially the mind of Christ, all the knowledge I had laboriously accumulated was as nothing by comparison. God responded to my cry to be able to see clearly as I saw in His presence by repeating word for word from a passage I didn't even know was in the Bible until I looked it up during lunch break. It was a passage from Isaiah, which says:

"I will bring the blind by a way they did not know; I will lead them in paths they have not known. I will make darkness light before them, and crooked places straight. These things I will do for them, and not forsake them." (Isa 42:16)

I reluctantly conceded to His reply, consoling myself with the expectation that it would not be long before He would finish His work in me, and then He would be able to use me to make Christ known as I had known Him during those three months. However, I soon discovered that a little while for God is not the same as a little while for us. As the months turned into years the promise seemed farther and farther from ever coming to fulfillment. I discovered that the greatest trials were those which followed, rather than preceded, my open heavens encounter. There were moments in which I felt that the heavens were opening again, only to discover that instead He was only giving me strength for the next valley.

I have always been painfully timid, preferring not to speak in public. Yet he placed me in pastoral ministry where I am always up-front speaking. There have been occasions in which the Spirit of the Lord has anointed me to preach a message. Those moments have been a joyful experience but all too few and far between. In a thousand ways He has been working death in me, and thousands of times I have despaired of my own abilities. Often, I have wanted to crawl into a hole somewhere and just disappear after fumbling through a message I couldn't even logically follow myself, let alone hope that the congregation should understand it. But each time, I remind myself of what He promised, and I have learned not to doubt in the dark what I saw clearly in the light of His presence.

Little by little I am discovering that the same truths that I learned in His presence during that three-month encounter are clearly set forth in the Scriptures. Paul explains how our minds need to be transformed to align with what we know to be true in Him:

*"But **you have not so learned Christ, 21 if indeed you have heard Him and have been taught by Him, as the truth is in Jesus**: 22 that you put off, concerning your former conduct, the old man which grows corrupt according to the deceitful lusts, 23 and be renewed in the spirit of your mind, 24 and that you put on*

the new man which was created according to God, in true righteousness and holiness." (Eph 4:20-24)

If we have not learned Christ, having been taught by Him as the truth is in Jesus, we may be experts in the Scriptures, and even memorize them as did the Pharisees, without understanding that, from Genesis to Revelation, the Scriptures point us to Jesus. The words of Jesus to the Scribes and Pharisees are still true of too many of us to this day:

"You search the Scriptures, for in them you think you have eternal life; and these are they which testify of Me. But you are not willing to come to Me that you may have life." (John 5:39,40)

All too many, even within the Body of Christ, are not walking in Christ as they began in Him and are seeking to find life through their own efforts *(Col 2:6-10)*. Many, as I did, are trying to live according to the Scriptures, but they miss the import of the Scriptures: The testimony of Jesus is the very spirit or essence of the inspired Word of God *(Rev 19:10)*. If you do not see Jesus as the focal point and the source of all life and true godliness, you are not seeing the Scriptures with the mind of Christ. We may be sincere and dedicated to rightly dividing the Word of God, but if we are relying on our natural mind of the flesh, we will never see the truth, as it is in Christ. We must look to the Holy Spirit to reveal to us the mind of Christ through our new spirit. The natural or *soulish* mind of the flesh cannot perceive spiritual realities:

*"But the natural (psuquikos – "soulish") man **does not receive the things of the Spirit of God**, for they are foolishness to him; nor can he know them, because they are spiritually discerned. 15 But **he who is spiritual judges all things**, yet he himself is rightly judged by no one." (1Cor 2:14-15)*

*"It is the Spirit who gives life; **the flesh profits nothing. The words that I speak to you are spirit**, and they are life." (John 6:63)*

The words of God are spirit words, which must be revealed through our spirit in communion with the Spirit of God. The soulish man, who depends upon his own understanding and his carnal senses, will never come to know the truth as it is in Christ.

Chapter four
Entire Sanctification

*"Now **may the God of peace Himself sanctify you completely;** and may your whole **spirit, soul,** and **body** be preserved blameless at the coming of our Lord Jesus Christ. 24 He who calls you is faithful, who also will do it." (1Thess 5:23-24)*

Having seen clearly the distinction between body, soul and spirit, we can now consider what is involved in our sanctification. The above passage begins and closes expressing God's commitment and faithfulness, to Himself completely sanctify us, not only in spirit, but also in soul and in body. It says that God is *"preserving"* us in order to present us blameless at the coming of the Lord Jesus Christ for us. The word translated *"preserved"* here is *teréo which means "to keep, guard, or watch over."* It expresses the Father's supervision and oversight of our sanctification process, having already predestined us to be conformed to the image of His Son *(Rom 8:29).*

The word *"sanctify"* is from the same root word as *"holy,"* and primarily means *"to set-apart."* God is holy or *set apart* from all of His creation. Holiness, when referring to us, speaks of us being *set-apart* – set apart *for* God and *from* sin and the world. There are three areas of the sanctification of our entire person: 1) In the past, our **spirit** *was* sanctified upon receiving Christ and being born again, 2) In the present, our **soul** *is being* sanctified to become just like Christ, even as our spirit is already holy and just like Christ and 3) In the future, our physical **body** *will be* instantly sanctified, being glorified at the coming of our Lord Jesus Christ, when we shall receive a body just like His. All three areas of sanctification are necessary in order to see the Lord in His glory. The author of Hebrews says:

"Pursue peace with all people, and holiness, without which no one will see the Lord." (Heb 12:14)

Here we see that peace and holiness are necessary prerequisites to see the Lord. Although our born again spirit was created in true righteousness and holiness in a moment's time, there is still a holiness to pursue. This is a truth that many grace teachers do not take into account. However, that being said, it must be made clear that the entire sanctification of all of His born again elect is guaranteed by God himself. Paul says in 1Thessalonians 5:24, concerning our entire sanctification: *"He who calls you is faithful, **who also will do it**."* Peter says essentially the same thing but with an additional element added:

*"But may the **God of all grace**, who called us to His eternal glory by Christ Jesus, **after you have suffered** a while, perfect, establish, strengthen, and settle you. 11 **To Him be the glory and the dominion forever and ever. Amen.**" (1Peter 5:10-11)*

Here again we see that God is the sanctifier and we are those being sanctified. However, Peter presents a truth that many grace teachers do not mention - God uses suffering to accomplish His sanctifying work in us. If we do not cooperate with Him by pursuing our ongoing sanctification along with Him, then He will intervene with corrective discipline, and therefore we should work out our salvation with fear and trembling, knowing that our Father God is a consuming fire, and that He will judge His people if they fail to judge themselves *(Php 1:12,13; Heb 12:29; 1Cor 11:30-32).*

If we are among His elect, and have truly been born again unto eternal life, then God has predestined us from eternity to be conformed to Christ's own image, and in His eyes we are already glorified:

*"And we know that all things work together for good to those who love God, to those who are the called according to His purpose. 29 For **whom He foreknew, He also predestined to be conformed to the image of His Son**, that He might be the firstborn among many brethren. 30 Moreover whom He predestined, these He also called; **whom He called, these He also justified; and whom He justified, these He also glorified.**" (Rom 8:28-30)*

Here we see that, from God's eternal perspective, all whom He foreknew have already been justified, conformed to Christ's image *and glorified* (past tense). Glorification, which refers to our resurrected and glorified bodies, is yet future to us but in God's mind it is already a certain and accomplished event. When it is God who begins the good work in you, you can rest assured that He will complete it. But we should still work out our salvation together with Him with fear and trembling, knowing that He disciplines every son He receives, in order that we may partake of His own holiness in our daily walk. He *gives grace* to us, enabling us to co-labor with Him in this process. However, it is a fearful thing to fall into Father God's hands when it comes to the correction of His obstinate children *(Heb 10:30,31; 12:5-11;28,29).*

When we see such passages as: *"Pursue peace with all people, and holiness, without which no one will see the Lord,"* we are often indoctrinated in such a way that we see them as a warning of God's rejection when in reality they express the opposite of rejection. These passages speak of *correction* - not *rejection.* They need to be read in their context where they are clearly speaking, not of our Father's *rejection* but of His *correction* of us, as His own children. Too often, these texts have been misinterpreted in such a way as to lead one to believe they are warning of eternal rejection and exclusion from His presence. For example, subconsciously we read the text as if it said: *"Pursue peace with all people, and holiness, without which no one will **EVER** see the Lord."*

We need to cast off all the false doctrines and erroneous mind-sets which are not biblical, but rather are a hangover from the Dark Ages. We need to be renewed in the spirit of our minds. We have a truly good Father who is absolutely committed to bringing all His children into a complete holiness, so they may see Him as He is and live before Him, no matter how difficult of a child they may be.

Many present our earthly fathers as being more committed to the proper upbringing of their children than Father God is. That is a Dark Ages mentality, and a distortion of the Father's heart, as revealed in Jesus' life and ministry. If you feel more secure with your earthly father than your heavenly Father, you need a fresh revelation of the true Father heart of God towards you.

In order to comprehend the sanctification of our entire person, spirit, soul and body, we will consider what the Scriptures have to say concerning sanctification, past, present and future.

Past-tense Sanctification in our Spirit

We have already seen much concerning the past-tense sanctification of our spirit, which was perfect in holiness and complete from the moment we were born of the Spirit of God. This sanctification is a done deal which cannot be improved upon, nor taken from. Any truly born again believer already has the very life of

Christ in his spirit, and possesses His eternal life. Jesus said of His sheep:

> *"And **I give them eternal life**, and **they shall never perish**; neither shall anyone snatch them out of My hand. 29 My Father, who has given them to Me, is greater than all; and **no one is able to snatch them out of My Father's hand**. 30 I and My Father are one." (John 10:28-30)*

As to our spirit, we are already one with the Lord, inseparably united to Him. His perfection is our perfection, His perfect holiness and righteousness are already ours in our spirits and cannot be improved upon. Our spirit is as infinite in perfection as Christ Himself. By His sacrifice, made once for all, we were perfected forever:

> *"By that will (will of God {v.9}) **we have been sanctified** through the offering of the body of Jesus Christ **once for all**.... 14 For by one offering **He has perfected forever** those who are being sanctified." (Heb 10:10,14)*

Here we see that our past sanctification perfected us forever. Those who have been sanctified in verse 10, have been perfected forever, according to verse 14. When it says that He *"has perfected forever those who **are being sanctified"*** in the latter part of verse 14, he is not contradicting what he already said in verse 10. One who has already been sanctified and perfected forever in their spirit cannot continue being sanctified in their spirit since it is already perfect.

The present tense, passive *"being sanctified,"* could either have reference to our soul, which continues to undergo a process of sanctification throughout our entire lives, or it could also have reference to each individual who successively becomes sanctified the moment they believe on Christ for salvation. In either case, we know that it is only our spirits which have already been perfected forever, since our souls are still in the process of sanctification. We also see later in Hebrews that it is only our spirit which has been made perfect:

> *"But you **have come** (past perfect tense) to Mount Zion and to the city of the living God, the heavenly Jerusalem, to an innumerable company of angels, 23 to the general assembly and church of the firstborn who are registered in heaven, to God the Judge of all, **to***

__the spirits__ of just men made perfect, 24 to Jesus the Mediator of the new covenant, and to the blood of sprinkling that speaks better things than that of Abel." (Heb 12:22-24)

Here the writer contrasts the Old Covenant relation with God, with the New Covenant relationship we now enjoy as born again believers. We are now already registered in heaven as those forming the Church of *the firstborn ones (pl.)*. And, having been perfected forever by the once for all sacrifice of Christ, we are now among the **spirits of just men made perfect**. As the firstborn ones, it is our spirit which is already just and perfect - not our soul. Through the inseparable union of our spirit with Christ, we are as perfect and complete as Christ himself in our spirit:

*"For in Him dwells all the fullness of the Godhead bodily; 10 **and you are complete in Him**..." (Col 2:9-10)*

We are now as fully accepted by the Father as the Son, because we are now one spirit with Him:

*"just as He chose us in Him before the foundation of the world, that we should be holy and without blame before Him in love, 5 having predestined us to adoption as sons by Jesus Christ to Himself, according to the good pleasure of His will, 6 to the praise of the glory of His grace, by which **He made us accepted in the Beloved**. 7 In Him we have redemption through His blood, the forgiveness of sins, according to the riches of His grace." (Eph 1:4-7)*

Note that the Father *made us* accepted, holy and without blame before Him – we did not make ourselves acceptable. We have already been made holy, without blame and accepted (past tense) – not *becoming* holy and acceptable and without blame before Him. That this is referring to our perfect spirit and not our soul, is evident when we see admonitions to *"be perfect." (James 1:4; 2Cor 12:9; Rom 12:2; Col 4:12; 2Cor 7:1, etc.)*. In our soul we still need sanctification and renewal. Contrary to what many grace teachers would say, not everything we think, decide and feel in our soul is acceptable to the Lord. Not everything we do in our flesh is acceptable to Him. It is our spirit that has already been made perfect forever.

The word *"accepted"* in Ephesians 4:6, is really a weak translation of the Greek word *charitáo,* which is the verb form of the word for *"grace"* – *(charis).* It literally means "to favor or to grace," and is only used in one other occasion in the New Testament in reference to Mary where Luke says: *"And having come in, the angel said to her, 'Rejoice,* **highly favored one** *(charitáo), the Lord is with you; blessed are you among women!" (Luke 1:28).* Our spirit, as a new creation in Christ, is not merely acceptable to God but *highly favored* by Him.

Our spirit is inseparably united to Christ, and therefore our spirit cannot sin. To the degree that we set our minds on the things of the Spirit, and walk in the spirit, we will live lives free from sin. According to John, it is because of our born again spirit, that those of us who have been born of God can no longer practice sin:

"Whoever has been born of God does not sin, **for His seed remains in him***; and he cannot sin, because he has been born of God. 10 In this the children of God and the children of the devil are manifest: Whoever does not practice righteousness is not of God, nor is he who does not love his brother." (1John 3:9,10)*

Here again, the King James Version mistranslates the passage, leaving out an important verb in verse nine. The verse, as translated, leaves out the verb *poiéo,* which means *"to do, commit or practice."* This has led many to doubt their salvation, because, no matter how devoted one may be, we all still sin. John establishes that fact in the first chapter of this same epistle: *"If we say that we have no sin, we deceive ourselves, and the truth is not in us…. 10 If we say that we have not sinned, we make Him a liar, and His word is not in us." (1John 1:8,10).* Obviously, in chapter three, he is not saying the opposite of what he just said in chapter one. When one includes the Greek verb *poiéo,* which in its present continuous form means *"to continually do or practice,"* and when one also sees that the phrase *"he cannot sin"* is also present continuous *("cannot be sinning"),* it becomes obvious that John is not teaching sinless perfection. The Greek scholar Kenneth Wuest, although rather wordy, correctly translates the true sense of the passage:

"Everyone who has been born out of God with the present result that he is a born-one of God **does not habitually commit sin** *because His seed remains in him. And* **he is not able habitually**

to sin, because out of God he has been born with the present result that he is a born-one of God." (1John 3:9 EPT)

This passage says that the reason we can no longer practice sin is because God's *seed* remains in us. Many commentators reduce the import of the word *"seed,"* saying that the expression *"His seed,"* is merely speaking of God's *"life principal."* The Greek word for *"seed"* is *sperma* from which we get the word "sperm." John says the reason we cannot continue to practice sin is because we have God's *sperma* in us. Being someone's seed in the Scriptures speaks of more than a mere *"principal."* It is speaking of the very lineage or spiritual DNA or genes of God (defining "seed" in modern terms). It is to have His very life – to be a partaker the divine nature of God himself. It is more than some theoretical "principal" – it is experiencing the very life and nature of God himself.

In what sense can it be said that God's seed abides in us? That which is born of Spirit is spirit. Therefore, His seed refers to our regenerated spirit, which was recreated perfect in true righteousness and holiness, and not our body or soul. It is our spirit that has the very life of Christ. If our spirit has truly been born of God, John says that it will result in a life that no longer walks in sin. We, as born again believers, cannot continue to sin in our soul, using our bodies as instruments of unrighteousness.

It is because of the fact that only our spirit has been born of the Spirit that Jesus said that our worship of God must originate in our spirit, and not our soul: *"God is Spirit, and those who worship Him must worship in spirit and truth." (John 4:24).* It is the only means we have to truly contemplate and worship God, who is an invisible Spirit.

That is not to say that the soul and body are unaffected in true worship - quite the contrary. I have learned that when our spirit is released to express itself in true worship of God, our emotions and thoughts are also enraptured in worship and our body also follows suit, often with tears, laughter, the lifting of hands, dance or prostration. However, on the contrary, we may cry, laugh, dance or prostrate ourselves from our souls, without it springing up from our spirit. We cannot bypass our spirits and truly worship God. Sadly, there is much soulish, carnal worship within many churches. Only those who are spiritual, walking according to the spirit, are able to discern the difference.

Present-tense Sanctification of our Soul

"Most assuredly, I say to you, unless a grain of wheat falls into the ground and dies, it remains alone; but if it dies, it produces much grain (karpós – "fruit"). 25 **He who loves his life** *(psuque – "soul")* **will lose it** *(apolumi – "lose or destroy")*, **and he who hates his life** *(psuque – "soul")* **in this world will keep it for eternal life***." (John 12:24-25)*

Sanctification of our soul, in contrast to the once and for all sanctification of our spirit upon being regenerated, is a present ongoing process. Failure to recognize this distinction has resulted in confusion for many, and a lack of holiness in the lives of some within the grace movement. Whenever the Scriptures speak of us as already holy or sanctified, past-tense, it is referring to our spirit which has already been created anew in perfect holiness before God. On the other hand, when we see reference to a holiness that God is working out in us in the present-tense, it is referring to the sanctification of our soul, which also indirectly affects our bodies.

In the illustration of the seed, given by Jesus, we see that the soul is as the outer shell which encases the true seed within, which is our new living spirit. Although the translators obscure the import of the passage by translating "soul" *(psuque)* as "life," and the Greek word *apolumi* as *"lose,"* rather than *"destroy,"* we see that what Jesus is saying here is that the soul-life (life lived dominated by the soul) must be taken into death or destroyed, just as the outer shell of a seed must be removed, in order that the new life of the spirit may break forth and bear fruit.

Many mistakenly think that to "lose or destroy" *(apolumi)* means to "lose forever" or "annihilate." However, that is not what the word expresses. The word *apolumi* simply means *"to undergo a change of state"* or *"to lose, (usually only to be found later)."* We see that meaning here in reference to the soul. It is not lost forever, or annihilated, but rather *kept* by allowing it to be destroyed and restored: *"he who hates and loses or destroys his soul* **will keep it***."* Jesus is saying that we must let go of our soul-life as we knew it in Adam and allow God to destroy it or *change its state*, only in order to finally restore it to us in the end, when it is renewed and subject to our new spirit which is already one with Christ.

70

Nothing in all of God's creation is annihilated or lost forever to God. Jesus said that He came to seek and save that which was lost *(Matt 18:11-14)*. Paul says that *"of Him and through Him and **to Him** (eis "into Him") are **all** things." (Rom 11:36)*. The words translated *"lost"* and *"perish"* in Matthew 18 are the same Greek word *apolumi* which we saw above. If Jesus said that He came to save that which is lost and that He leaves the ninety-nine to seek the one lost sheep *until He finds it*, do you think that any would be lost to Him forever? Certainly not! *Apolumi,* meaning to lose or destroy, is only temporary, until it is either found or restored, as the case may be. In the same manner, if we allow God to take our soul-life into death in this present time, He promises that we will *keep* our souls (i.e. they will be saved or restored whole) when the process of death to the self-life is complete:

> *"Then He said to them all, "If anyone desires to come after Me, **let him deny himself**, and **take up his cross daily**, and follow Me. 24 For **whoever desires to save his life** (psuque – "soul") **will lose it** (apolumi), but whoever **loses** (apolumi) his life (psuque) for My sake **will save it**." (Luke 9:23,24)*

This is the ongoing process of the sanctification of our souls. It involves suffering, and is often so painful and humbling that many seek to elude it, but God is committed to sanctifying each and every one of His children entirely, and we only prolong the process by our lack of submission:

> *"Therefore humble yourselves under the mighty hand of God, that He may exalt you in due time…. may the God of all grace, who called us to His eternal glory by Christ Jesus, **after you have suffered** a while, **perfect, establish, strengthen, and settle you**. 11 To Him be the glory and the dominion forever and ever. Amen." (1Peter 5:6,10,11)*

This is referring to the painful process of the destruction of the outer-man, the self-life or the soul, in order that our perfect, newly created spirit, in union with Christ, may then reign over our souls, with our bodies becoming instruments of righteousness, rather than instruments of sin as they were in Adam. Although I didn't understand it yet at the time, this is what the Lord was calling me to, through my three-month open heavens encounter with Him, in 1982.

Our former lives in Adam were limited to the realm of the soul, living according to our own feelings, will and reason, and walking after the desires of the flesh. The soul-life does not die, giving way to the spirit, easily. As one renowned minister said: *"The path of spiritual progress is marked by the bloody foot-prints of wounded self-love."*

In the present grace revolution, we must guard against embracing a crossless form of Christianity, which would seek to eliminate the need to daily take up our cross and follow Jesus. Many grace teachers would even go so far as to say that Jesus' teaching concerning the way of the cross is not for us today. They claim that it is Old Covenant teaching which does not apply to us under the New Covenant. However, we see elsewhere, as in 1Peter 5:10, that suffering and self-denial are still an essential part of the sanctification of our entire man in the New Covenant epistles as well, and is not only found in the teachings of Jesus.

Paul said that he was *"always carrying about in the body the dying of the Lord Jesus, that the life of Jesus also may be manifested in our body. For we who live are **always delivered to death for Jesus' sake**, **that the life of Jesus also may be manifested in our mortal flesh**."* (2Cor 4:10,11). He is speaking not only of his own experience, but of the daily death to the soulish self-life *we all* must undergo, in order that the new life of Jesus may be manifested in our mortal flesh, through our born again spirit.

Also, in Revelation it speaks of what is required in order to be a New Covenant overcomer: *"And they overcame him by the blood of the Lamb and by the word of their testimony, **and they did not love their lives** (psuque – "soul") **to the death**."* (Rev 12:11). So we see that one cannot escape our death to the old adamic soul-life by simply relegating the teachings of Jesus to the Old Covenant.

Paul said concerning suffering: *"This is a faithful saying: For if we died with Him, we shall also live with Him. If we endure (suffering, v.9), we shall also reign with Him. If we deny Him, He also will deny us."* (2Tim 2:11-12). If we are united with Him in His death we are saved and will live with Him. However, if we would reign with Him, we must suffer with Him, because His reign is a spiritual reign, and only those who are spiritual, having died to the soulish self-life, are qualified to reign in His spiritual kingdom. He says the same to the Romans:

*"The Spirit Himself bears witness with our spirit that we are children (teknon) of God, 17 and if children, then heirs — heirs of God and joint heirs with Christ, **if indeed we suffer with Him, that we may also be glorified together**." 18 For I consider that the sufferings of this present time are not worthy to be compared with the glory which shall be revealed in us.19 For the earnest expectation of the creation eagerly waits for the revealing of the sons (huios – "mature sons") of God." (Rom 8:16-19)*

Some argue that Jesus suffered so that we would not have to suffer. This is true if we are speaking of His suffering on the cross in our place for our sins. He suffered the due penalty for our sins so that we would not have to suffer their penalty. However, in order to be qualified to reign with Him, we must go on from being forgiven little children to become mature sons. When it comes to the ongoing sanctification of our soul and the death of our self-life, there is no way to get around the need to take up our cross daily and follow Him:

*"Therefore, since Christ suffered for us in the flesh, arm yourselves also with the same mind, for **he who has suffered in the flesh has ceased from sin**, 2 that he no longer should live the rest of his time in the flesh for the lusts of men, but for the will of God." (1Peter 4:1-2)*

In Adam, being dead to God, our souls were programmed to live according to the will of the flesh, since without God, the flesh and the world were all that we were alive to. But now that we have been made alive in our spirits in relation to God, our souls need to be reprogrammed by the renewing of our minds, in order that we may now live according to the will of God, according to our new spirit and no longer for ourselves, according to the flesh and the world. There is presently a war going on for the dominance of our souls:

*"Beloved, I beg you as sojourners and pilgrims, abstain from fleshly lusts which **war against the soul**." (1Peter 2:11)*

The flesh and the world seek to dominate and influence our souls as it did before, but we are now first and foremost a newly created spirit, and our spirit's desires are according to the will of God. Our spirit, in union with Christ, must be released to control our soul and bodies according to God's will:

"For the flesh lusts against the Spirit, and the Spirit against the flesh; and these are contrary to one another, so that you do not do the things that you wish." (Gal 5:17)

Our present sanctification consists in reprogramming of our souls through the renewing of our minds according to the will of God, living and walking in our mortal bodies according to the dictates of the spirit, and no longer according to the dictates of the soul and the flesh:

*"For **this is the will of God, your sanctification**: that you should abstain from sexual immorality; 4 **that each of you should know how to possess his own vessel** (physical body) **in sanctification and honor."** (1Thess 4:3-4)*

The carnal, soulish believer has a new spirit, just as the spiritual Christian. Both the spiritual believer and the soulish believer are united with God in their spirit. However, in the case of the unsanctified carnal believer, his spirit is not able to influence his insubordinate soul and do the will of God through his body. Since his soul still minds the things of the flesh and of this world instead of the things of the spirit, God is not able to live out His life through the carnal, soulish Christian. The predominant influence in his life is external - of the world, which appeals to the appetites of his flesh.

In contrast, the spiritual believer has subjected his soul to his spirit, being renewed in his mind and controlled by input from God, rather than from the world and the flesh. In this manner, his entire man, spirit, soul and body, becomes aligned with the will of God. His intellect, will and emotions, are all subject to the will of God through his spirit, and the result is that the life of Christ may now be manifest in his mortal body. In this manner our souls are presently being sanctified or set-apart from sin unto God.

Post-mortem Sanctification

Doubtlessly, to any thoughtful student of Scripture the question arises: If we must attain to complete sanctification, body, soul and spirit, in order to see the Lord, then what about those believers who die before attaining to that sanctification, without which no one will see the Lord? There are those who are saved just before death, while many weaker or more difficult children of God, even after many years, have died without attaining to full sanctification. I believe that

74

we must all honestly admit that none of us will arrive at the goal of complete sanctification this side of the grave. If death marks the end of the sanctification of our souls, how then will we ever be able to see the Lord?

Many have wrongly assumed that the sanctification of the believer ends at death. If that were true, none of us would ever be able to see Him, since not one of us will ever achieve absolute perfection of our souls in this life. Paul explained that there will be a post-mortem cleansing by fire, which all believers must undergo at death:

> "For no other foundation can anyone lay than that which is laid, which is Jesus Christ. 12 Now if anyone builds on this foundation with gold, silver, precious stones, wood, hay, straw, 13 **each one's work will become clear; for the Day will declare it, because it will be revealed by fire; and the fire will test each one's work, of what sort it is**. 14 If anyone's work which he has built on it endures, he will receive a reward. 15 **If anyone's work is burned, he will suffer loss; but he himself will be saved, yet so as through fire**." (1Cor 3:11-15)

Note that this is a post-mortem fire that those who have built their lives upon Christ, the only foundation, must pass through. When does this testing by fire take place? Many commentators argue that it is on the day of Christ's Second Coming. While that would be true for those living at the time of His coming, I believe that this particular "day" is referring to the day we appear before the Lord, whether through death, or at the moment we are caught up to meet the Lord in His coming. To be absent from the body is to be present with our Lord who is a consuming fire, and on that day His fire will consume every dead work from us as believers. However, our salvation is not in question at this judgment. Even if all we have ever done is consumed in this fire, Paul says that we will nevertheless be saved, yet as through fire. I believe that this fire of His presence is what will perfect that which may be lacking in our entire sanctification. For some, it will be very painful. They will be greatly ashamed and will suffer great loss of rewards. On the other hand, those who have maintained an abiding relationship will at that time receive the crown of rejoicing (1Thess 2:19,20).

Jesus, teaching His disciples, said to them: "For everyone will be salted with (in) fire." (Mark 9:49 NASU). Both fire and salt are purifying agents and Jesus says that all, without exception, will have to pass through the fire of purification. The fire is not a literal fire, as many have thought, but rather is a fire which consumes that which is evil, or useless - it is a purifying fire.

That day, when the fire consumes all that is worthless in our lives, must take place either individually at the moment of death, or collectively with all those alive, who will be caught up to meet the Lord on the day of His Second Coming. All must pass through this fire, because to be absent from the body is to be present with the Lord, and without complete holiness, body, soul and spirit, no one can see Him. John says concerning this moment:

> "Beloved, now we are children of God; and it has not yet been revealed what we shall be, but we know that **when He is revealed, we shall be like Him, for we shall see Him as He is.** 3 And **everyone who has this hope in Him purifies himself,** just as He is pure." (1John 3:2-3)

We know that we will be like Him when He appears, because without holiness no one will be able to look upon the Lord, and yet we shall see Him as He is in all His glory. This hope or expectation is a motive for present sanctification in preparation for the day of His revealing. Knowing that we will soon see Him as He is, motivates us to abide in Him in order that we may have confidence and not be ashamed on that day, whether it be the day of our death or the day of His Second Coming:

> "And now, little children, abide in Him, that when He appears, we may have confidence and not be ashamed before Him at His coming." (1John 2:28)

Premature Death – A Disciplinary Measure

We also see in the New Testament that there are some believers whose lives are cut short due to failure to judge sin in their own lives. When we persistently fail to judge sin in our lives there comes a point where the Father, in corrective judgment, removes his disobedient child through death for post-mortem discipline, in order that he should not be condemned with the world:

> "But let a man examine himself, and so let him eat of the bread and drink of the cup. 29 For he who eats and drinks in an unworthy manner eats and drinks judgment to himself, not discerning the

*Lord's body. 30 **For this reason many are weak and sick among you, and many sleep**. 31 For if we would judge ourselves, we would not be judged. 32 But **when we are judged, we are chastened by the Lord, that we may not be condemned with the world**." (1Cor 11:28-32)*

Very few grace teachers would accept that God would resort to such disciplinary measures as sicknesses, tribulation or much less a premature death, but that is exactly what we find in the New Testament. The writer of Hebrews warns saying:

*"...The Lord will judge **His people**. It is a fearful thing to fall into the hands of the living God." (Heb 10:30-31)*

However, even when He takes one of His children in premature death, as we see above, it is not for *condemnation* but for *correction*. They are not removed in condemnation, but rather in order *that they may not be condemned with the world*. There is no condemnation for those who are in Christ Jesus *(Rom 8:1)*. Even in the extreme case of premature death, it is a removal for *correction*, not *condemnation*.

We who have been born of God are sons by birth – not by adoption, as some mistakenly believe. [5] One who is a son by birth

---

[5] Many have mistakenly applied the western concept of adoption to the Greek word *huiothesia* translating it "adoption". The word simply means "to place as an adult son" *(it is a compound word composed of* "son" - *huios* and *tithemi* - "to place")*. Both Vines Expository Dictionary of New Testament Words and Doctor C.I. Scofield make the following comments concerning the meaning of the term *huiothesia:*

"In Eph 1:5 they are said to have been foreordained unto 'adoption as sons' through Jesus Christ, RV; the KJV, 'adoption of children' is a mistranslation and misleading. God does not 'adopt' believers as children; they are begotten as such by His Holy Spirit through faith. 'Adoption' is a term involving the dignity of the relationship of believers as sons; it is not a putting into the family by spiritual birth, but a putting into the position of sons. In Rom 8:23 the 'adoption' of the believer is set forth as still future, as it there includes the redemption of the body, when the living will be changed and those who have fallen asleep will be raised." (Vines Expository Dictionary of New Testament Words)

"Adoption (huiothesia, 'placing as a son') is not so much a word of relationship as of position. The believer's relation to God as a child results from the new birth (John 1:12, 13), whereas adoption is the act

can never cease to be the son of his father, no matter what may occur. This is even more the case with God's own children, who were born again with His own eternal life.

We also see this same post-mortem discipline with a premature death implied in 1John five, which speaks of some brethren who persist in sin to the point where God will not even answer the prayers of others for their healing, and takes them in death:

*"Now this is the confidence that we have in Him, that if we ask anything according to His will, He hears us. 15 And if we know that He hears us, whatever we ask, we know that we have the petitions that we have asked of Him. 16 If anyone sees **his brother** sinning a sin which does not lead to death, he will ask, and He will give him life for **those who commit sin not leading to death. There is sin leading to death**. I do not say that he should pray about that. 17 All unrighteousness is sin, and there is sin not leading to death." (1John 5:14-17)*

After speaking of the assurance that we have that God hears and answers our prayers, John continues by clarifying that he isn't saying that God will always answer the prayer for the life of a brother who continues in sin, because it may be God's will to take him out of the way for correction. A literal translation of verses 16 and 17 is helpful in understanding what John was actually saying:

*"If anyone sees his **brother <u>sinning sin</u> not leading to death**, he will ask, and **He will give him life for those not sinning to death. There is sin leading to death. I do not say that he should pray about that**. 17 All unrighteousness is sin, and **there is sin not leading to death." (1Jn 5:16,17)*

What John is saying is that some brethren may persist in sin *(sinning sin)* to the point where God determines to take them in

---

*of God whereby one already a child is, through redemption from the law, **placed in the position of an adult son** (Gal. 4:1-5). The indwelling Spirit gives the realization of this in the believer's present experience (Gal. 4:6); but **the full manifestation of the believer's sonship** awaits the resurrection change and translation of saints, which is called 'the redemption of the body' (Rom. 8:23; 1Thess. 4:14-17; Eph. 1:14; 1John 3:2) (emphasis added)."* (Scofield Reference Bible) death. If that is the case, even our prayers for them will not spare them from a premature death. However, it doesn't result in their condemnation, but rather the Father takes them aside for postmortem correction *in order that they should not be condemned with the world* and that He may present them faultless in the day of the Lord Jesus (i.e., before the Second Coming and the first resurrection). *(Jude 24; 1Cor 11:32, cf. 1Cor 5:5).*

In chapter three of John's first epistle he says that those who are born of God cannot persist in sin. Why is that so? The first and most obvious reason we have already considered - our essential nature was changed in the new birth. We now have God's own nature in our newborn spirit, having been born of God. Now that we are a new creation in Christ, when we do sin, we are acting contrary to our true nature. We are no longer sinners by nature, but we are the born ones of God and partakers of His own divine nature.

However, as John stated in the first two chapters of 1John, even though we, as God's children have been forgiven, we still often sin, acting contrary to who we now are in Christ. Some who persist in sin require the Father's disciplinary intervention. The Father is committed to presenting each and every elect born again believer as a chaste virgin to Christ in the day of the Lord when He returns. He is not the kind of Father who will stand by and allow His children to continue acting in a manner harmful to themselves and others, sinning in defiance to His authority over them. That is the second reason why those born of God cannot persist in sin - the loving Father will not permit it.

However, no matter how obstinate his elect born-ones may be, His calling and election are without repentance. He will never "un-son" us. He who has called us is faithful, and, come what may, He will complete the good work which He began in us:

> *"Now may the God of peace Himself sanctify you completely; and may your whole spirit, soul, and body be **preserved blameless at the coming of our Lord Jesus Christ**. 24 **He who calls you is faithful, <u>who also will do it</u>**." (1Thess 5:23-24)*

If God has chosen you to salvation in this age, you have already been glorified as far as He is concerned *(Rom 8:28-30).* Even if we are faithless, He remains faithful - He cannot deny Himself. If He has begun a good work in you, rest assured that He will bring it to completion before the day of Jesus Christ when you will be presented as Christ's bride:

> *"being confident of this very thing, that He who has begun a good work in you will complete it until the day of Jesus Christ." (Phil 1:6)*

Even if He has to deliver you over to Satan for the destruction of your flesh, or even take you out of this world prematurely for disciplinary judgment, He is able, willing and faithful to make you ready in time for the day of Christ, and He himself will do it, if you are truly among the firstborn of His elect children *(Heb 12:23)*.

Our Father Administers Corporal Punishment

> *"And you have forgotten the exhortation which speaks to you as to sons: 'My son, do not despise the **chastening** of the Lord, nor be discouraged when you are **rebuked** by Him; 6 **For whom the Lord loves He chastens**, and **scourges** every son whom He receives.' If you endure chastening, God deals with you as with sons; for what son is there whom a father does not chasten? 8 But if you are without chastening, of which all have become partakers, then you are illegitimate and not sons. 9 Furthermore, we have had human fathers who corrected us, and we paid them respect. Shall we not much more readily be in subjection to the **Father of spirits** and live? 10 For they indeed for a few days chastened us as seemed best to them, but He for our profit, that we may be partakers of His holiness. 11 Now no chastening seems to be joyful for the present, but **painful**; nevertheless, afterward it yields the peaceable fruit of righteousness to those who have been trained by it." (Heb 12:5-11)*

What I see as a very grave error within the grace movement is the tendency of some to reject any Scriptures making reference to the Father's discipline which go beyond mere warnings. I believe this is due, at least in part, to the mindset among the millennials that sees all physical, corporal punishment as unloving and abusive. However, in the Scriptures we see corporal discipline to be a loving action: *"He who spares his rod hates his son, but he who loves him disciplines him promptly." (Prov 13:24)*.

The few grace teachers I have found who comment on Hebrews 12:5-11 at all, avoid any mention of the word *"scourges,"* insisting that God would never take a hand to His children, even when they stubbornly fail to take heed to His reproofs. They say that, because God loves us, He would never resort to physical discipline such as sickness, hardships or tribulation in order to correct us. But quite to the contrary, what we see here is that we shouldn't lose heart when He rebukes, chastens and scourges us because it is actually an indication that He does love us – He loves us enough to take whatever measures are necessary for our correction.

I don't believe that He himself causes the sickness or calamity but rather grants permission to Satan, within set limits, just as He did with Peter or Job. But just as was the case with Peter and Job, His discipline afterwards *yields the peaceable fruit of righteousness to those who have been trained by it.* As Jesus said to the church of Thyatira concerning a prophetess among them that was leading many of them into fornication:

*"And **I gave her time to repent** of her sexual immorality, and she did not repent. 22 Indeed **I will cast her into a sickbed, and those who commit adultery with her into great tribulation,** unless they repent of their deeds." (Rev 2:21,22)*

Here we see that the Lord reproves us, giving us opportunities to repent. But if we do not take heed to His verbal correction, He will progressively administer more and more severe discipline, as He sees necessary, in order that we might repent. Any good earthly parent would do the same with their own children. Some however, who wish to continue living according to the sinful passions of their flesh, seek out teachers that present the Father as though He were a permissive parent who tolerates whatever His children happen to be into and never goes beyond mere words to correct us *(2Tim 4:2-4).* That, however, is not paternal love, but neglect and indifference.

We have a truly good Father who will never leave us because of *who we are,* but neither will He leave us *as we are.* He is faithful and committed to sanctify us entirely, conforming us to the image of His Son, Jesus Christ, in order to present us to Him as a chaste virgin on that day. And if we would love life and see good days, we must learn to pursue holiness together with Him, in loving submission under His mighty hand *(1Peter 5:6,10,11).*

Future-tense Sanctification of our Physical Bodies

The final sanctification of our bodies is still future, not taking place until the Second Coming of Christ. Many through the centuries have mistakenly thought that we can sanctify our physical bodies in a direct manner in this life. This has led some to such extremes as prohibiting foods, self-flagellation, vows of chastity and even dismemberment, in an attempt to sanctify their physical bodies. But Paul makes it clear that such measures are of no value against the desires of the flesh:

> "Therefore, if you died with Christ from the basic principles of the world, why, as though living in the world, do you subject yourselves to regulations — 21 'Do not touch, do not taste, do not handle,' 22 which all concern things which perish with the using — according to the commandments and doctrines of men? 23 **These things indeed have an appearance of wisdom in self-imposed religion, false humility, and neglect of the body, but <u>are of no value against the indulgence of the flesh</u>**." (Col 2:20-23)

Paul warns that in the last days some will depart from the faith of Jesus, and instead of walking in the Spirit, they will impose a form of legalistic asceticism:

> "Now the Spirit expressly says that in latter times some will depart from the faith, giving heed to deceiving spirits and doctrines of demons, 2 speaking lies in hypocrisy, having their own conscience seared with a hot iron, 3 **forbidding to marry, and commanding to abstain from foods** which God created to be received with thanksgiving by those who believe and know the truth." (1 Tim 4:1-3)

The body, as a physiological organism, is neutral, being neither good nor evil. It can either be used as an instrument of sin or an instrument of righteousness, depending upon whom we present it to. The sanctification, present-tense, is that of the soul, and only affects the body indirectly, converting it into a useful vessel for the Lord's use. Jesus explained that sin does not originate in our physical bodies, but from within:

> "And He said, 'What comes out of a man, that defiles a man. 21 For **from within, out of the heart of men, proceed evil** thoughts,

adulteries, fornications, murders, 22 thefts, covetousness, wickedness, deceit, lewdness, an evil eye, blasphemy, pride, foolishness. 23 **All these evil things <u>come from within</u>** *and defile a man." (Mark 7:20-23)*

We cannot fight flesh with flesh. Jesus said that *the flesh profits nothing.* The fleshly deeds of the body can only be mortified indirectly through the Spirit when our soul is subject to our spirit. Only in this way can the life of Jesus be manifested in our mortal bodies instead of the desires of the flesh. The law of the Spirit of life in Christ makes us free from the law of sin and death:

"For the law of the Spirit of life in Christ Jesus has made me free from the law of sin and death. Therefore, brethren, we are debtors — not to the flesh, to live according to the flesh. 13 For if you live according to the flesh you will die; but **if <u>by the Spirit</u> you put to death the deeds of the body, you will live.***" (Rom 8:2; 12,13)*

Future Sanctification of our Bodies

Even as our human spirits *were sanctified* – having been recreated perfect in holiness and eternal *in a moment's time* in the past when we were reborn, so also our physical bodies *will be sanctified* – they will become perfect and separate from sin's effects and made immortal *in a moment's time,* in the future, at Christ's return:

"Now this I say, brethren, that flesh and blood cannot inherit the kingdom of God; nor does corruption inherit incorruption. 51 Behold, I tell you a mystery: We shall not all sleep, but we shall all be changed - 52 **in a moment, in the twinkling of an eye**, *at the last trumpet. For the trumpet will sound, and the dead will be raised incorruptible, and* **we shall be changed**. *53* **For this corruptible must put on incorruption, and this mortal must put on immortality**. *54 So when this corruptible has put on incorruption, and this mortal has put on immortality, then shall be brought to pass the saying that is written: 'Death is swallowed up in victory." (1Cor 15:50-54)*

This flesh and blood physical body is not designed in such a way as to withstand the unmitigated glory of God and His kingdom. Both Daniel and John, even though they were godly men, fell as dead men under the weight of God's glory *(Daniel 10:8; Rev 1:17).* In the case of Daniel, it wasn't even God himself but simply an angel sent from the Lord's presence. We must receive an immortal glorified body in order to be able to see Him in all His glory. The glory of Christ in His coming will be so great that if we were not glorified before being caught up with Him at His coming, our physical bodies would literally be consumed:

*"...until our Lord Jesus Christ's appearing, 15 which He will manifest in His own time, He who is the blessed and only Potentate, the King of kings and Lord of lords, 16 who alone has immortality, **dwelling in unapproachable light, whom no man has seen or can see**, to whom be honor and everlasting power. Amen." (1 Tim 6:14-16)*

Of the Antichrist, it is said that he will be physically destroyed by the brightness of His coming *(2Thess 2:8)*. Until now, He has always veiled His glory because of our frail humanity, but then we shall see Him as He is, and in order for that to be possible, we must first receive our immortal glorified bodies *(1John 3:2)*.

Although we cannot even begin to comprehend the glory which shall be revealed in us, we have already received a foretaste of His glory, since we have received the firstfruits of the Spirit, and we groan in eager anticipation for *"the adoption"* – (i.e. our manifestation as sons of God, when our bodies will be redeemed and transformed):

*"For we know that the whole creation groans and labors with birth pangs together until now. Not only that, but we also who have the firstfruits of the Spirit, even **we ourselves groan within ourselves, eagerly waiting for the adoption, the redemption of our body**." (Rom 8:22,23; cf. 2Cor 5:1-5)*

Although we have not yet physically seen Him, and we do not yet know how we shall be on that glorious day, the Spirit within us reveals to those who are spiritual the unimaginable glory reserved for us in heavenly places:

*"But as it is written: 'Eye has not seen, nor ear heard, nor have entered into the heart of man the things which God has prepared for those who love Him.' 10 **But God has revealed them to us through His Spirit**. For the Spirit searches all things, yes, the deep things of God." (1Cor 2:9-11)*

In conclusion, we have seen that God, in His grace, is the one sanctifying us completely - spirit, soul and body. If we pursue holiness together with Him in the present time, availing ourselves of the grace He gives, walking in the Spirit and not in the flesh, it will be well with us and we will see good days. But ultimately God himself is committed to perfecting the work of sanctification which He began in each and every one of His elect, and one way or another He is going to present every one of us as His children to Jesus Christ, as a chaste virgin in the day of His coming.

Chapter five

Conviction, Confession and Repentance

Much of the controversy concerning the grace teaching has to do with their application of these three words: conviction, confession and repentance, when used in reference to sin. Some grace teachers argue that these actions are no longer necessary for us as Christians, since we have already been forgiven once and for all and have already been sanctified in the past. They reason that God can no longer convict us of our sins because He no longer even sees our sins under the New Covenant. They would say that confessing sins already forgiven is actually committing the sin of unbelief, because such a person does not believe that all his sins have already been forgiven. Any repentance of sin in the life of a believer (especially if it includes sorrow for sin), is seen as *sin consciousness*, rather than *Christ consciousness,* and must be repented of (no pun intended).

Their arguments seem logical at first glance. However, in order to argue their point, they must avoid a great body of Scripture. Failing to recognize the truths pertaining to the sanctification of the entire man – spirit, soul and body; past, present and future, many of them tend to only site the passages referring to what God has done for us in the past, while denying or ignoring the present tense passages referring to our present relationship with God and our ongoing, present-tense sanctification.

This view of the Christian life tends to limit grace to what God has done and does *for* the believer, ignoring what His grace is doing in and *through* us when we walk in communion with Him. It is true that we have been forgiven all our sins - past, present and future and that we have been made perfect forever. It is also true that we have been justified, and all our sins have been remitted, never again to be held against us. *"There is therefore now no condemnation to those who are in Christ Jesus." (Rom 8:1).*

But does it follow that God therefore never reproves us when we justify sin in our lives? Is it now no longer needful for us to repent or change our minds about sins – confessing them to God? Clearly, once justified, we will never again be condemned for our sins, but doesn't our ongoing communion with God, of necessity, require agreeing with Him concerning sin (confession)? Is it not true that, in any relationship, confession or agreement is necessary in order to maintain communion? Is it wrong for us to ask God to forgive us when we have acted against His will? *"Can two walk together, unless they are agreed?" (Amos 3:3).*

It is understandable that many who have lived under the heavy yoke of legalism, with its resultant paralyzing sense of guilt and condemnation, should be drawn to the message as presented by the grace movement. I believe that the grace movement presents the truth as far as a once for all forgiveness is concerned. However, many are left at risk of receiving the grace of God in vain by neglecting the present-tense aspect of sanctification. The grace-walk involves *walking* in grace and *growing* in grace. It requires our participation, working according to His grace which mightily works in and through us *(Col 1:29; 1Cor 15:10)*. To me, much grace teaching leaves many mulling around inside the gate, when God, by His grace, would lead us on from strength to strength, from faith to faith and from glory to glory.

Does God Convict His Children of Sin?

*"And when He has come, **He will convict the world** of **sin**, and of **righteousness**, and of **judgment**: 9 of sin, because they do not believe in Me; 10 of righteousness, because I go to My Father and you see Me no more; 11 of judgment, because the ruler of this world is judged" (John 16:8-11)*

Nearly all grace teachers present the conviction of the Holy Spirit as being negative and condemnatory when it refers to His conviction of sin. Some would even say that when He convicts someone of sin, they become a convict, or a condemned person. However, even when conviction is used with reference to the world, the Holy Spirit's convicting is meant to bring salvation – not condemnation. The Father did not send His Son into the world to condemn the world, but to save the world through Him *(John 3:17)*. Jesus came to reconcile the world - not bring a judicial conviction against it *(John 12:47)*.

Whenever the word "convict" (Gr. *alegko*) is used outside of court, person to person, it is not to be understood as *conviction* in a judicial sense, but rather as convincing arguments meant to correct, persuade or convince of the truth for the benefit of the one being convinced. Actually, the word is never used in the judicial condemnatory sense in the New Testament, and for that reason "convict" is a misleading rendering of the word. It is often used in a correctional context, and therefore is translated as "a rebuke." However, it is also used to convince someone concerning positive truth, as seen in this very passage in John 16:10,11. Jesus said that the Holy Spirit will convince the world of three things: 1) He will convince the world of *sin*, because they do not believe in Jesus, 2) He will convince the world of *righteousness* and 3) He will convince the world of *judgment* because the ruler of this world has been judged.

It should be emphasized that in all three instances the convincing ministry of the Holy Spirit is for salvation – not condemnation. Its purpose is salvific and positive – not condemnatory and negative. It is intended to remove the veil from our eyes, first by revealing our sin – especially that of not believing in Jesus. Until the Spirit convinces concerning sin, many are deluded into thinking that they are not really sinners in need of salvation through Christ. Contrary to what many grace teachers say, even the law and the conscience cannot convince us of our true condition outside of Christ without the conviction of the Holy Spirit, which unveils our true depravity and need.

After convincing us of our sin and need of the Savior, the Spirit takes us to the next step – He convinces us of righteousness. In what sense can it be said that the Spirit convinces us of righteousness? What righteousness? Our own righteousness or the lack thereof? No. The righteousness that He convinces us of, after convincing us of our sin and need of Christ, is the righteousness of God which is received (not "achieved") by faith alone, offered freely by God's grace which is in Jesus Christ, who is now our righteousness. Because He left us in order to present His own blood to the Father as a propitiation for our sins on the heavenly mercy-seat, all believing on Him have now been clothed with His own righteousness.

However, the convincing of the Holy Spirit does not stop with revealing to us the righteousness which is now ours through our union with Christ. He not only clothed us with His own righteousness when He rose and ascended to the Father, but through His death He also destroyed the authority of the devil over the lives of those who are Christ's. The Holy Spirit, after convincing to us our sinful condition and presenting to us the righteousness of the ascended Christ who now lives in us, proceeds to convince us of Christ's victory in judgment against the ruler of this world. So, the Spirit first convinces us of our sin and need of Jesus; then He convinces us that Christ's own righteousness is now ours; and finally, He convinces us that we are now free from Satan's dominion because the ruler of this world has already been judged.

This same progressive revelation is seen in the book of Romans which is the most complete presentation of the gospel found anywhere in the New Testament. Paul begins by revealing that all are sinners – both the Jews who have the Law and the Gentiles who only have their conscience. Then after convincing all of their sinful state and the total depravity and inability to save themselves, he presents to them the righteousness of God in Christ, received as a gift of God's grace *(Rom 3:21 - 5:20)*. Then he convinces us that we are no longer bound to sin and the devil, as we formerly were in Adam *(Rom 6:1 - 8:11)*.

When we receive power to be His witnesses, the Holy Spirit in communion with us, convinces the world of sin, righteousness, and judgment (not our judgment but the judgment against the ruler of this world). Our commission is to preach repentance and remission of sins together with the Holy Spirit *(Luke 24:47-49)*.

However, what the grace teachers insist upon is that, although the Spirit convinces the world of sin, He does not convince God's children of sin. It is true that, in the judicial sense, the Spirit will never convict us in the sense of bringing a charge against us. However, it is not true that God never convinces or reproves us *(alegko)* concerning sin in our lives.

One prominent grace teacher challenged his readers to find one text to substantiate the claim that the Spirit convicts God's children. He seemed very confident that God is nowhere said *to convict* His children in the New Testament. However, his confidence was based upon a translation and not the original Greek text. The same Greek word, *alegko,* is indeed used more than once to describe God's corrective rebuke of His own:

> *"And you have forgotten the exhortation which speaks to you as to sons: '**My son**, do not despise the chastening of the Lord, nor be discouraged when you are **rebuked** (alegko) **by Him**; 6 For whom the Lord loves He chastens, and scourges **every son** whom He receives." (Heb 12:5-6)*

*"As many as I love, I **rebuke** (alegko) and chasten. Therefore be zealous and repent." (Rev 3:19)*

*"All Scripture is given by inspiration of God, and is profitable for doctrine, for **reproof** (alegmos), for correction, for instruction in righteousness, 17 that **the man of God** may be complete, thoroughly equipped for every good work." (2 Tim 3:16,17)*

Here, in these passages, we see the same word used in reference to the Lord's corrective reproofs of His own children. If the Spirit convicts the world of sin for their own benefit, bringing man to see his need of salvation, how much more will He reprove His own sons when they persist in sin! In Scripture, rebukes, correction and even physical discipline, are seen as an indication that the parent who administers the discipline loves his child and will do whatever is necessary for their proper development.

The problem, as I see it, is that many within the grace movement are the younger generation who were brought up in a society in which corrective discipline is seen as unloving, and it has been banned from the school system and even forbidden in the home. The results can be seen in our postmodern society as prophesied by Paul *(2Tim 3:1-7)*. Father God, however, is uncompromisingly committed to conforming His children into the image of His Son, and He will not be bound by the societal norms of our generation.

Many grace teachers, in a strange twist of logic, would claim that the second reference to the conviction of the Spirit, mentioned by Jesus in John 16, has reference to us as believers instead of the world. Without any regard for sentence structure, they dissect the sentence making it out to say:

*"And when He has come, He will convict **the world** of **sin**, and (us **believers**) of **righteousness**, and (the **world**) of **judgment**: 9 of sin, because they (the **world**) do not believe in Me; 10 (and you **believers**) of righteousness, because I go to My Father and you see Me no more; 11 of judgment (of the **world**), because the ruler of this world is judged" (John 16:8-11)*

According to this misinterpretation, the direct object receiving conviction is the world at the beginning of the sentence when He speaks of sin and also at the end when He speaks of judgment, but in the middle of the sentence the direct object switches somehow to us as believers, whom He only convinces of our righteousness in Christ. However, just a basic knowledge of sentence structure would refute this interpretation. The subject of the action "shall convict" is the Holy Spirit. The direct object receiving the action of conviction is *"the world"* throughout the entire sentence. The Holy Spirit convicts the world of all three – sin, righteousness and judgment. It may be helpful for some to repeat the main clause before each prepositional phrase in the following manner:

"And when He has come,
He will convict the WORLD *of* **sin***, and of* **righteousness***, and of* **judgment***:*

> 9 **He will convict the WORLD** *of* **sin***,*
>> *because they do not believe in Me;*
> 10 **He will convict the WORLD** *of* **righteousness***,*
>> *because I go to My Father and you see Me no more;*
> 11 **He will convict the WORLD** *of* **judgment***,*
>> *because the ruler of this world is judged" (John 16:8-11)*

While it is true that the Holy Spirit, through the Word, convinces us, as believers, that we are the righteousness of God in Christ Jesus, this passage is speaking exclusively of the Holy Spirit's work in *the world*, bringing about the salvation of mankind.

Therefore, we have seen that the Greek word *alegko* should be translated as "convince or reprove" instead of the judicial term "convict" when referring to the Holy Spirit's saving and sanctifying influence. We have seen that the world is convinced of sin, righteousness and judgment in John 16:8-11, and we also as believers are seen as being *rebuked* or *convinced* of sin by the Father, the Son and the Holy Spirit, in passages such as *(Heb 12:5-6; Rev 3:19; Rev 2:16,17)*. Conviction of sin is not only for the world, but is also carried out, as necessary, for the correction of God's own children.

Confessing our Sins for Forgiveness

The grace teachers rightly point out that we have already been forgiven of all sin - past, present and future at the cross. All of our sins have been remitted, and God says that He will remember them no more *(Matt 26:28; Heb 10:17,18)*. If we were to stop with these passages, the logical conclusion would be that, since all sins are forgiven and no longer remembered by God, all confession of sin in the present is superfluous at best, and unbelief at worst.

However, this simple conclusion is complicated by two texts which explicitly present confession as necessary for our forgiveness:

*"If we say that we have no sin, we deceive ourselves, and the truth is not in us. 9 **If we confess our sins, He is faithful and just to forgive us our sins** and to cleanse us from all unrighteousness." (1John 1:8,9)*

*"Is anyone among you sick? Let him call for the elders of the church, and let them pray over him, anointing him with oil in the name of the Lord; 15 and the prayer offered in faith will restore the one who is sick, and the Lord will raise him up, and **if he has committed sins, they will be forgiven him. 16 Therefore, confess your sins to one another, and pray for one another, so that you may be healed." (James 5:14-16 NASB)** [6]*

These particular passages present a seeming paradox: If all our sins have been forgiven - past, present and future, why then do we still need to confess them for forgiveness and healing? This is further complicated by The Lord's Prayer, which hinges the Father's forgiveness of us upon our forgiveness of each other:

*"And **forgive** us our debts, as **we forgive** our debtors. 13 And do not lead us into temptation, but deliver us from the evil one. For Yours is the kingdom and the power and the glory forever. Amen. 14 'For if you forgive men their trespasses, your heavenly Father will also forgive you. 15 But **if you do not forgive** men their trespasses, **neither will your Father forgive** your trespasses." (Matt 6:12-15)*

Grace teachers typically attempt to explain these passages in such a way as to have no application to us as believers today. The following is a consideration of their interpretation of each of the above texts.

---

[6] Some Greek manuscripts read *"trespasses"* in verse 16 instead of "sins."

The Lord's Prayer and Forgiveness

First, they relegate the Lord's Prayer to the prior dispensation of the Old Covenant Law, saying that the Lord's discourse concerning conditional forgiveness does not apply to us today under the New Covenant. They say that under the Old Covenant they had to forgive to be forgiven, whereas under the New Covenant we are told to forgive as we have already been forgiven *(Eph 4:32; Col 3:13)*.

While it is true that in one sense God's forgiveness precedes our forgiveness under the New Covenant, we also see that in another sense we will receive God's mercy according to our mercy shown towards others *(James 2:13)*. One must be discerning when separating the old from the new in the teachings of Jesus. Obviously, we cannot easily write off the Lord's Prayer as Old Covenant when the same truth taught by Jesus in the Lord's Prayer is repeated again in the New Testament epistles, as we see in James 2:13. Rather than invalidating the Word of God in order to defend our particular doctrine, we should look for an understanding which allows all Scripture to be understood in its plain normal sense.

Forgiveness and Healing

Most grace teachers prefer not to tackle James 5:14-16. As was the case with Jesus in His earthly ministry, James connects forgiveness with healing when he says: *"the prayer offered in faith will restore the **one who is sick**, and the Lord will raise him up, and **if he has committed sins, they will be forgiven him**."* This verse speaks of a future forgiveness, received through the prayers of others, resulting in the person being forgiven and healed of his sickness. It is assumed in this passage that sickness can sometimes be inflicted as judgment upon a believer who persistently refuses to judge sin in his own life *(see also 1Cor 11:30-32; 1John 5:16,17)*.

It is obviously God who here forgives the individual who is sick due to unjudged sin in his life. Therefore, there must be a sense in which we, as His own justified and forgiven children, still need to continue receiving an ongoing forgiveness from the Father. If we believe that all Scripture is inspired of God, we cannot simply pick and choose - we must seek to find the harmonious truth of Scripture taken as a whole.

"If we confess" Refers to the Early Gnostics

John says, **if we confess our sins, He is faithful and just to forgive us our sins** and to *cleanse us from all unrighteousness. (1John 1:9).* Almost all Christians, prior to the grace movement, have understood this promise as referring to the believer who confesses his sins to God in order to be forgiven by Him. However, grace teachers point to the fact that just a few verses later John tells believers that their sins have already been forgiven:

> *"I am writing to you, little children, because your sins have been forgiven you for His name's sake." (1John 2:12 NASU)* [7]

John says here that our sins *"have been forgiven"* (perfect tense, passive voice), meaning that our sins were forgiven in the past with the result that we continue in a forgiven state. This agrees with other passages where we see that Christ's once for all sacrifice perfected us forever *(Heb 10:14; Col 2:13).* Grace teachers argue that it would be contradictory to say that we have been forgiven our sins in chapter two, and then insist that we must continue confessing our sins in order to receive forgiveness in chapter one. How do they explain this apparent contradiction?

Grace teachers seek to establish that John's use of *"we"* and *"us"* in chapter one is not referring to us as believers, but to unbelieving Gnostics who denied that they had sin, or that Christ came in flesh. They argue that John was politely including himself, as referring to mankind in general. Instead of saying to them *"if you say,"* etc., which could have been considered condescending and insensitive, he said *"If we say."*

This is something that we often do out of courtesy when we wish to convince someone. While it is true that *"we"* at the beginning of the chapter has reference to "we the twelve disciples," in verse six, beginning with the phrase *"If we say,"* he is politely speaking primarily to the Gnostics, since they, rather than John, were the ones who claimed to have fellowship with God while denying that they had sin. One can observe this shift in verse six, where the *"we"* is no longer referring to "we the apostles" but "we in general."

---

[7] I quote from the NASU because it correctly translates the perfect passive *"have been forgiven."*

*"That which was from the beginning, which **we** have heard, which **we** have seen with our eyes, which **we** have looked upon, and our hands have handled, concerning the Word of life — 2 the life was manifested, and **we** have seen, and bear witness, and declare **to you** that eternal life which was with the Father and was manifested **to us** — 3 that which **we** have seen and heard **we** declare **to you**, that **you also** may have fellowship **with us**; and truly **our** fellowship is with the Father and with His Son Jesus Christ. 4 And these things **we** write **to you** that **your** joy may be full. 5 This is the message which **we** have heard from Him and declare **to you**, that God is light and in Him is no darkness at all.
6 **If we say** that we have fellowship with Him, and walk in darkness, **we lie** and do not practice the truth.
7 But **if we** walk in the light as He is in the light, **we** have fellowship with one another, and the blood of Jesus Christ His Son cleanses **us** from all sin.
8 **If we say** that **we** have no sin, **we** deceive ourselves, and the truth is not in **us**. 9 If **we** confess **our** sins, He is faithful and just to forgive **us** our sins and to cleanse **us** from all unrighteousness.
10 **If we say** that **we** have not sinned, **we** make Him a liar, and His word is not in **us**."* (1John 1:1-10)

That John is countering some primitive form of Gnosticism is evident throughout the entire epistle. He first counters the Gnostic claim that the man, Jesus, was not Himself the Christ, but simply a man upon whom the "Christ spirit" descended at baptism, only to leave His body before He suffered and died upon the cross. He counters that claim in verses one and two by emphasizing that they tangibly heard and handled the eternal Word which was with the Father, and was manifested in a tangible body, thereby negating the Gnostic error that claimed that Jesus wasn't Himself the Christ incarnate.

In verses two through four, he invites the Gnostics to fellowship with them by embracing this truth, thereby enabling them to enjoy fellowship with the Father and His Son Jesus Christ. The very name, Jesus Christ, was rejected by the Gnostics, since they denied that Jesus was Himself the Christ. Whoever denies that Jesus was the Son of God himself in flesh, does not have the Father. Later in his epistle, he is a little more straightforward, saying that anyone who denies that Jesus is the Christ is not only a liar, but is antichrist and is without the Father or the Son *(1John 2:22,23)*.

In verse five, John tells them that Jesus had taught them (the disciples) that God is absolute light, with no darkness at all. Then in verses six through the end of the chapter, he politely counters their erroneous belief concerning sin. The Libertine Gnostics were of the belief that man is a perfect eternal spirit, who abides in divine light. They claimed that the sins committed in their flesh could not contaminate them, no matter how much they sinned in their physical bodies.

Even as they made a false dichotomy between the physical man, Jesus, and the divine Christ-spirit, they also made a false dichotomy between our physical bodies and our eternal spirits. They held to the view that their spirit-man is eternal, and they simply incarnated temporarily in flesh, and how they lived in the flesh had no effect upon their perfect spirit.

Even as their view of Christ was antichrist, so also their view of man was antichrist. The Bible reveals that our spirit was dead towards God because of sin. Our spirits had to be born again by the Spirit of God. When our spirit is reborn, becoming one with Christ, we can no longer continue to sin and walk in darkness in our bodies. According to John, one who continues to practice sin does so because he has not been born of God *(1John 3:9)*. Their view of man, as was their view of Christ, is antichrist, since it denies the need of Christ's redemption for our sins, and it also denies that we must be born anew in our spirit - being made one spirit with the resurrected Christ. Only because of our inseparable union with Christ do we now have His righteousness and eternal life in our spirit. As Paul says:

"And if Christ is in you, the body is dead because of sin, but the Spirit (spirit) is life because of righteousness." (Rom 8:10)

In 1John 1:6 it says that the one who claims to have fellowship with God, who is light, while at the same time physically walking in the darkness, is living a lie. On the other hand, if we walk in the light with our physical bodies, we enjoy fellowship with one another *(i.e. with each other and with the Father and with His Son Jesus Christ {v.3})*, and the blood of Jesus Christ His Son continually cleanses us from all sin *(present tense) {v. 7}*.

If a Libertine Gnostic were to be confronted with sin in his life, he would deny that he had sin, attributing it to his flesh, which, according to him, was not him, but only his temporary body. In verse eight John

97

confronts their refusal to own up to their own sin, saying that anyone who denies that they have sin is self-deluded and void of the truth.

That brings us to the verse under consideration: *"If we confess our sins, He is faithful and just to forgive us our sins and to cleanse us from all unrighteousness."* The word *"confess"* is *homologéo* (a compound word: *homo* – *"same"* and *légo* – *"to say"*). It means *"to say the same thing"* or *"come into agreement with."* It is the opposite of their denial of sin that we saw in the previous verse. John is saying to them: "If you come into agreement with God concerning your sin, He is faithful and just to forgive and cleanse you, but if you continue to deny your sin He cannot forgive and cleanse you. What's worse, your denial makes God out to be a liar, and His word is not in you." *(v. 9,10).*

"If we confess" also applies to Us

I believe the grace teachers are correct in their assertion that John had the early Libertine Gnostics in mind throughout the entire epistle. Phrases such as: *"If we say," "He who says," "He who..."* and *"Whoever..."* all address different errors introduced into the Church by early Gnostics who later became known as the Libertine Gnostics. However, demonstrating that each of these introductory phrases exposes the distinct false doctrines of the Gnostics, does not mean that they have no relevance to us. Every one of them has just as much application to us as it did to the Gnostics. That is why John could truthfully say: *"If we...,* rather than *"if you."*

Going back to the beginning of John's first chapter, we should ask whether or not what John was saying has application to us as well, or whether it is something only applicable to the Gnostics. What about walking in the light as opposed to darkness? Does that apply to us or only to the Gnostics? John says:

> *"**If we say** that we have fellowship with Him, and **walk in darkness**, **we lie** and do not practice the truth. But **if we walk in the light** as He is in the light, **we have fellowship** with one another, and the blood of Jesus Christ His Son cleanses **us** from all sin." (1John 1:6,7)*

The question that must be answered from Scripture is this: Is it possible for us, as children of the light, to walk in darkness as well? Would that affect our fellowship with God who is light? Do we need to repent, confess our sins and return to the light in fellowship for forgiveness and cleansing? Grace teachers would deny all the above, saying that it only is applicable to Gnostics or unbelievers, but what do the Scriptures have to say?

What Fellowship has Light with Darkness?

Grace teachers confuse our *identity* as children of light with our daily *walk* in the light. They say that as children of light we cannot walk in darkness, so 1John 1:6 cannot apply to us. However, in the New Testament we are exhorted to walk according to who we now really are in Christ:

*"For you were once darkness, but **now you are light** in the Lord. **Walk as children of light**" (Eph 5:8)*

Here we see Paul exhorting us, as children of light, to walk in the light, even as He is in the light, just as John says in 1John 1:7. Paul also says that we must cast off darkness and put on light, *walking* as in the day:

*"The night is far spent, the day is at hand. Therefore **let us cast off** the works of **darkness**, and **let us put on** the armor of **light**. 13 **Let us walk** properly, **as in the day**, not in revelry and drunkenness, not in lewdness and lust, not in strife and envy. 14 But put on the Lord Jesus Christ, and make no provision for the flesh, to fulfill its lusts." (Rom 13:12-14)*

They also argue that our fellowship with God cannot be broken. According to them, since He doesn't see our sin, we are always in fellowship with Him. Therefore, they say that John here was simply calling on the Gnostics to confess for salvation and come into a perfect fellowship with God that cannot be interrupted by our sin. But is it true that our fellowship with the Lord cannot be interrupted because of darkness in our lives? Again, we see that fellowship requires that we walk in agreement with God:

*"Do not be unequally yoked together with unbelievers. For what fellowship has righteousness with lawlessness? And **what communion** (koinonía – "fellowship") **has light with darkness?** 15 And what accord has Christ with Belial? Or what part has a believer with an unbeliever? 16 And what agreement has the temple of God with idols? For you are the temple of the living God.*

*As God has said: 'I will dwell in them and walk among them. I will be their God, and they shall be My people.' 17 Therefore '***Come out from among them and be separate***, says the Lord. **Do not touch what is unclean, and I will receive you**.' 18 'I will be a Father to you, and you shall be My sons and daughters, says the Lord Almighty.' 7:1 Therefore, having these promises, beloved, let us cleanse ourselves from all filthiness of the flesh and spirit, perfecting holiness in the fear of God." (2Cor 6:14-7:1)*

*"Therefore submit to God. Resist the devil and he will flee from you. 8 **Draw near to God and He will draw near to you**. Cleanse your hands, you sinners; and purify your hearts, you double-minded." (James 4:7,8)*

Other New Covenant admonitions could be cited, but these should be sufficient to demonstrate that, though we are not Gnostics, 1John 1:6,7 has application to us, even though we are children of light. We must daily *walk* in the light, and actively maintain fellowship with God and one another. If we *walk* in the light as He is in the light, we have fellowship with one another, and the blood of Jesus Christ His Son continually cleanses us of all sin (present continuous action). But if we detour into darkness to hide our sin, our fellowship with the Lord is interrupted until we come back into agreement with God, confessing our sins and returning to the light of His presence. When we do that, John says, He is faithful and just to forgive us, and cleanse us from all unrighteousness.

Relationships broken by Sin require Confession and Forgiveness in order to continue

What many grace teachers fail to take into account, downplay or outright deny, is that in any society there are two distinct types of forgiveness – *judicial* forgiveness and *relational* forgiveness. In a court of law, justice must be executed, even if the offender is the judges' own son. Under a justice system, every offense must receive its just penalty. God is both Father and Judge, but His forgiveness as Judge is not the same as His forgiveness as Father.

God, as our Father and Judge, could not simply forgive us without inflicting upon us the just penalty for our offenses against justice. As the Father of all He loves us, but as Judge He could not righteously execute justice and simply overlook our offenses. God's solution is found in the mystery of our redemption through the cross. Christ, on the cross, paid in full the due penalty for sin once and for all, and God can now be just, and at the same time justify the ungodly, because Christ became the propitiatory sacrifice for all *(Rom 3:25,26; 1John 2:2)*. Therefore, whenever we see our forgiveness presented as a *done deal,* it is referring to this judicial forgiveness:

*"And you, being dead in your trespasses and the uncircumcision of your flesh, He has made alive together with Him, **having forgiven you all trespasses**, 14 having wiped out the handwriting of requirements that was against us, which was contrary to us. And He has taken it out of the way, having nailed it to the cross." (Col 2:13-15)*

Whenever we see references to a forgiveness brought about once and for all, as in the above verse, it is referring to *judicial* forgiveness, not *relational* forgiveness. The language of this verse is legal. Such terms as justification, propitiation, atonement and redemption all indicate a judicial forgiveness, accomplished by the redemptive work of the cross, which satisfies the exacting requirements of God's justice and holiness, once and for all.

Relational forgiveness, on the other hand, is ongoing. Such terms as justify, propitiate, atone, etc. have no place in this form of forgiveness. Rather, what we see is an ongoing forgiveness, where confession is followed by restoration and cleansing – not a repeated justification or propitiation.

If you commit a crime, you are taken before the judge, and if you are found guilty, you will be condemned to a sentence, no matter how remorseful you may be. However, for those of us who are in Christ Jesus, there is now no condemnation (*katacrisis* - "condemnatory sentence"). *(Rom 8:1)*. When we are in sin, we are not walking in the light, and our fellowship with the Father is broken. But since, through the new birth, we are now related to Him in a paternal relationship and not a judicial one, we may be disciplined by Him, but we will never, ever be condemned by Him as our Judge.

Failure to recognize this important distinction has only brought confusion to many of God's children, plunging them into the bondage of relating to God as Judge - trying to *justify* their actions and *propitiate* for their sins, instead of confessing them to their Father and allowing Him to take them into His arms and cleanse them from all sin.

The Lord's Prayer makes perfect sense once one understands that God's forgiveness of us or the withholding thereof is paternal and relational – not judicial:

*"**Forgive us our debts, as we forgive** our debtors. 13 And do not lead us into temptation, but deliver us from the evil one. For Yours is the kingdom and the power and the glory forever. Amen. 14 For if you forgive men their trespasses, **your heavenly FATHER** will also forgive you. 15 But **if you do not forgive** men their trespasses, **neither will YOUR FATHER** forgive your **trespasses**." (Matt 6:12-15)*

Note that Jesus here refers to God as *our Father,* and not as our judge. When the Scriptures speak of judicial forgiveness, it is just the opposite of what we see here. When speaking of judicial forgiveness, it is always in the past. We are told to forgive even as we *have already been forgiven* in Christ:

*"And be kind to one another, tenderhearted, **forgiving** one another, **even as God in Christ FORGAVE** you." (Eph 4:32)*

Most grace teachers, failing to acknowledge this important distinction between judicial forgiveness and paternal forgiveness, have excluded the Lord's Prayer, saying that it doesn't apply to us under the New Covenant. However, the same truth is presented in the New Testament epistles as well. In James, for example, we see forgiveness by God as being ongoing, and His mercy towards us conditioned upon our mercy towards others *(James 2:13; 5:14-16).* It should be obvious that it is referring to the kind of forgiveness we need in the family, in order to maintain communion and harmony.

There is another problem with limiting the confession of sins in 1John to the unsaved Gnostics, in addition to the fact that John includes us all when he says *"If **we** confess our sins, He is faithful and just to forgive us **our** sins and to cleanse **us** from all unrighteousness."* The Greek scholar A.T. Robertson rightly draws attention to the present tense of the verb *"confess."* He says: *"present active subjunctive of homologeoo, '**if we keep on confessing.**' Confession of sin to God and to one another (James 5:16) is urged*

102

throughout the New Testament." [8] The present tense of the verb *"confess"* implies that it is ongoing and relational and speaks of something more than the initial repentance and confession of sin at salvation.

In summary, although the grace teachers would deny it, our daily relationship with our heavenly Father requires confession whenever we willfully sin. They deny that there are two classes of forgiveness in the New Testament - *judicial* and *relational*. But the reality is that there is a forgiveness of sins, once for all, which justified us, and there is another ongoing forgiveness which we only receive when we forgive our enemies or confess our sins.

If we are consistently walking in the light as He is in the light, we have fellowship with Him, and although we may sin, it doesn't affect our communion, because the blood of Christ keeps on cleansing us from all sin *(v. 7)*. However, when we willfully sin and refuse to repent, we go into darkness in order that our deeds should not be reproved by the light *(John 3:20,21)*. And in that state of denial, our fellowship is interrupted, until we confess our sins to Him (i.e. come back into agreement with Him). Upon confessing our sin to Him, He immediately forgives us and cleanses us, just as any loving father would do with his son, as soon as he confesses his wrongdoing.

Repentance for Forgiveness of Sins

Repentance simply means, *"to reconsider or change one's mind."* (from *metanoéo* - *meta* *"change"* and *noéo* *"to think"*). True repentance first changes our way of perceiving things, sometimes through corrections and reproofs, but ideally through the daily renewing of our minds, as we grow in our understanding of the will of God *(Rom 12:2)*.

Grace teachers tend to show contempt for any call to repentance which is accompanied with a warning or rebuke. One prominent grace teacher comments concerning this:

"A mixed-grace preacher will use carrots ("Turn from sin if you want to see God") and sticks ("If you don't, you'll pay the

---

[8] Robertson's Word Pictures in the New Testament. Copyright © 1985 by Broadman Press.)

price"), but this is the way of the flesh, not faith. This sort of repentance will lead you to trust in your own repenting efforts and miss grace." [9]

Admittedly there is much fleshly repentance promoted within the traditional church which needs to be repented of. However, not every reproof, admonition or call to repentance, that warns of the consequences of not heeding it, is of the flesh. Jesus himself (after initiating the New Covenant) warns the churches of the consequences of failing to heed His call to repent of their sins:

*"Remember therefore from where you have fallen; **repent and do the first works, OR ELSE** I will come to you quickly and remove your lampstand from its place — **unless you repent**." (Rev 2:5)*

*"**Repent, OR ELSE** I will come to you quickly and will fight against them with the sword of My mouth." (Rev 2:16)*

*"And **I gave her time to repent** of her sexual immorality, and **she did not repent.** 22 **Indeed I will cast her into a sickbed**, and those who commit adultery with her into great tribulation, **UNLESS they repent** of their deeds." (Rev 2:21,22)*

*"Remember therefore how you have received and heard; **hold fast and repent**. Therefore **if you will not** watch, **I will come upon you as a thief**, and you will not know what hour I will come upon you." (Rev 3:3)*

Grace teachers tend to relegate all calls to repentance to the Old Covenant, insisting that it is now only the goodness of God which leads man to repentance. In order to establish their point, they often quote the last phrase of Romans 2:4 which reads, *"the goodness of God leads you to repentance."* However (apart from the fact that the phrase is part of a question - not an affirmation), reading the whole context we see that the goodness of God is not the only measure the Lord will resort to, if we remain obstinate:

---

[9] Ellis, Paul. The Hyper-Grace Gospel: A Response to Michael Brown and Those Opposed to the Modern Grace Message (Kindle Locations 685-687). KingsPress. Kindle Edition.

*"Or do you despise the riches of His goodness, forbearance, and longsuffering, not knowing that **the goodness of God leads you to repentance**? 5 **But in accordance with your hardness and your <u>impenitent heart</u>** you are treasuring up for yourself wrath in the day of wrath and revelation of the righteous judgment of God." (Rom 2:4-5)*

Here again, in context we see that the very passage they use against *"repent or else,"* actually teaches that very thing. While it is true that the goodness of God leads us to repentance, we can and often do, resist His goodness, hardening our hearts.

They also argue that repentance is not necessary for forgiveness. The author above quoted says: *"Repentance for the forgiveness of sins is an old covenant concept. It's doing (repenting) to get (forgiveness)."* [10] However, in the New Testament we continue to see repentance being a requirement for forgiveness, not only for an initial judicial forgiveness, as seen on the day of Pentecost, but also for relational forgiveness, as with Simon, who had believed on Christ, but later coveted the power Peter had, and offered him money for it, or the church of Thyatira which refused to repent of fornication:

*"**Repent** therefore and be converted, **that your sins may be blotted out**, so that times of refreshing may come from the presence of the Lord." (Acts 3:19)*

*"**Repent** therefore of this your wickedness, and pray God if perhaps the thought of your heart **may be forgiven** you." (Acts 8:22)"*

*"And I gave her **time to repent** of her **sexual immorality**, and **she did not repent**. 22 Indeed I will cast her into a sickbed, and those who commit adultery with her into great tribulation, **unless they repent of their deeds**." (Rev 2:21-22)*

In the first example, the repentance was at initial salvation, as would have been the case with the Gnostics John addressed, if they were to confess their sins. However, in the case of Simon and the

---

[10] Ellis, Paul. The Hyper-Grace Gospel: A Response to Michael Brown and Those Opposed to the Modern Grace Message (Kindle Locations 1717-1728). KingsPress. Kindle Edition.

believers in Thyatira, they were believers who nevertheless needed to repent for forgiveness of sins *(Acts 8:13).*

The truth of repentance for forgiveness is closely related to confession for forgiveness. If our sins have already been forgiven, why do I need to confess and repent of my sins in order to be forgiven? The answer to this question, as we saw earlier, is found in the distinction between judicial forgiveness and paternal, relational forgiveness which is extended to us when we confess and repent. For all practical purposes, repentance and confession are one and the same act, since true repentance or change of mind includes confession, or coming into agreement with God.

Finally, some grace teachers would say that repentance is simply a change of mind and should not involve sorrow. As one grace teacher says:

> *"...many of us have the impression that repentance is something that involves mourning and sorrow. However, that is not what the Word of God says. Repentance just means changing your mind."* [11]

While it is true that repentance is a change of mind, a *true* repentance inevitably results a change of conduct. Even as faith without a corresponding action is nothing more than mental assent, repentance which is a mere acknowledgment that one is wrong, is not true repentance. When the repentance (or change of mind) involves sin, and we realize that our actions have sorrowed and grieved God and others, lack of remorse on our part would indicate a disconnect – not true repentance. How can we not feel sorrow upon realizing that we have grieved the Holy Spirit within us, or hurt others?

However, grace teachers are correct in saying that sorrow, in and of itself, is not meritorious, and does not necessarily lead to repentance. There is much sorrow and grief in the world which does not produce repentance. Nevertheless, according to Paul, there is a godly sorrow that leads to true repentance:

---

[11] Prince, Joseph. Destined To Reign (Kindle Locations 3456-3457). . Kindle Edition.

*"Now I rejoice, not that you were made sorry, but that **your sorrow led to repentance**. For you were made sorry in a godly manner, that you might suffer loss from us in nothing. 10 **For godly sorrow produces repentance** leading to salvation, not to be regretted; **but the sorrow of the world produces death**. 11 For observe this very thing, that **you sorrowed in a godly manner**: What diligence it produced in you, what clearing of yourselves, what indignation, what fear, what vehement desire, what zeal, what vindication! In all things you proved yourselves to be clear in this matter."* *(2Cor 7:9-11)*

Godly sorrow comes when we see our sin as God sees it. Grace teachers have a problem with this because they believe that God doesn't even see our sin. But the fact that God does not count our sins against us does not mean that He isn't aware of them, and that He isn't grieved by them. The fact that there is now no more condemnation, doesn't mean that the Father will never take us to the woodshed if we continue to ignore His reproofs.

While sorrow, in and of itself, will not free us from our sins, the denial of sorrow, encouraged by some grace teachers, can cause us to sear our conscience and quench the Spirit to the point that we may actually become past feeling *(Eph 4:17-19)*. If you feel sorrow for your sin, it is not sinful. Allow that sorrow to produce in you a true repentance leading to godliness.

True Repentance is from Sin to God

Last but not least, I would like to emphasize that true repentance, which leads to godliness, is more than repenting of sin and turning from sin. If one stops there, he will be trapped in a vicious cycle of sin and failure, sorrow, repentance and resolutions, only to fail once again, falling into sin, being sorry, repenting and making new resolutions,… *ad infinitum*.

If we see repentance as simply turning from sin when we feel sorrow, we will never experience God's deliverance or salvation, because the flesh profits nothing against the power of indwelling sin. There must be a turning *from* sin *to* **God**, receiving His grace to help in time of need *(Heb 4:16)*.

We need to see that true repentance begins with a change of mind *(metanoéo),* and that transformation does not come by the will of the

107

flesh, but through the renewing of our minds. We need to understand that we truly have died with Christ to sin and have been raised with Him to newness of life. Grace is more than freeing us from sin: It is the very life of Christ lived out in our mortal bodies.

It should be obvious by now that while considering myself a part of the grace movement I part company with the majority of the grace teachers when it comes to their understanding of the points covered in this chapter. I see the Lord's reproofs or conviction of sin as an indication of His love and grace. Also, I see confession and repentance of sins as necessary in order to maintain an abiding relationship with Him. We are saved and forgiven once and for all, solely by His grace, but in our daily walk, we must keep ourselves in the grace of God, walking the straight and narrow grace walk *(Acts 13:43)*.

Chapter six

Grace Works

> *"But by the grace of God I am what I am, and His grace toward me was not in vain; but **I LABORED** more abundantly than they all, **yet not I, but the grace of God which was with me**." (1Cor 15:10)*

What both sides of the grace debate often overlook or minimize is the dynamic of grace. Mixed-grace teachers see grace as simply an auxiliary to the flesh, thereby empowering us to work for God. On the other hand, some grace teachers tend to reduce grace to the point of only referring to what God has done, or does *for us*, failing to lay sufficient emphasis upon what grace does *in and through us,* as we walk in communion with Him. Grace teachers are correct in seeing Jesus as being grace personified. Properly applying this truth to the above passage, we could state it in this manner: *"I labored more abundantly than they all, **yet not I, but Christ who is in me**." (cf. Gal 2:20).*

Two Distinct Kinds of Works

The New Testament presents two distinct kinds of works: 1) The *works of the flesh* or *dead works (Gal 5:19; Heb 6:1),* and 2) *New creation works* or *grace-works*, which are produced in our lives by God's grace as we abide in Christ *(Eph 2:10; Heb 13:20-21; Phil 2:12,13).*

The works of the flesh are works produced by us when we are either unbelievers or carnal fleshly Christians. A partial list of them is given by Paul in Galatians five:

> *"Now the works of the flesh are evident, which are: adultery, fornication, uncleanness, lewdness, 20 idolatry, sorcery, hatred, contentions, jealousies, outbursts of wrath, selfish ambitions, dissensions, heresies, 21 envy, murders, drunkenness, revelries, and the like; of which I tell you beforehand, just as I also told you in time past, that those who practice such things will not inherit the kingdom of God." (Gal 5:19-21)*

The truth is that no man, apart from Jesus Christ, has ever consistently obeyed the Law by his own self-efforts in the flesh. Even when we set out to keep the Law, the end results are all the infractions mentioned above. The flesh is not subject to the Law of God, nor can it be *(Rom 8:7)*. Paul, in Romans seven, says that the Law only serves to arouse our sinful passions *(Rom 7:5)*. He affirms the words of Jesus, *"the flesh profits nothing,"* concluding that, whether one is a believer or an unbeliever, the flesh is of no use when it comes to living a life of obedience to God:

> *"I know that **in me (that is, in my flesh) nothing good dwells**; for to will is present with me, but how to perform what is good I do not find. 19 For the good that I will to do, I do not do; but the evil I will not to do, that I practice." (Rom 7:18-19)*

Some seem to believe that, although unredeemed flesh cannot please God, "redeemed flesh" can. However, there is no such thing as "redeemed flesh." Our flesh was not redeemed at the cross – it was condemned and crucified on the cross in order that we may live unto God *(Gal 5:24; Rom 5:19,20)*. The works of the flesh – even those "good" works done *for* God, rather than *by* the power and leading of the resurrected Christ within us, are dead works and as worthless as filthy rags at best.

God, from the beginning, has ordained that we should walk in certain good works and He, by His own grace, motivates and empowers us to walk in them:

> *"For **by grace you have been saved through faith**, and that not of yourselves; it is the gift of God, 9 **not of works, lest anyone should boast**. 10 For **we are His workmanship, created in Christ Jesus for good works, which God prepared beforehand** that we should walk in them." (Eph 2:8-10)*

Our God has foreordained certain good works, tailor-made for each one of us to walk in. These works are not independently carried out *by* us, but rather lived out *in* us through Christ, who is now our life. The carnal believer is not necessarily one who is partaking of the evil branches of the forbidden tree. Any independent decision or action on our part constitutes a partaking of the tree of the knowledge of good and evil, rather than partaking of Jesus Christ – the Tree of Life.

Carnality often takes the form of legalism. Instead of an abiding relationship with Christ - our life, and receiving directives from Him, the legalist busies himself with a flurry of activity in an effort to do the works of God. Jesus Christ, the Son incarnate, taught us by His own example how we are to truly carry out the works of God:

*"Most assuredly, I say to you, **the Son can do nothing of Himself, but what He sees the Father do**; for whatever He does, the Son also does in like manner.* 20 *For the Father loves the Son, and **shows Him all things that He Himself does**; and He will show Him greater works than these, that you may marvel." (John 5:19,20)*

*"I must work the **works of Him** who sent Me." (John 9:4)*

*"Do you not believe that I am in the Father, and the Father in Me? The words that I speak to you I do not speak on My own authority; but **the Father who dwells in Me does the works**." (John 14:10)*

Jesus said that the works done in His body were not His works but the works of the Father. The Father who dwelt in Him did the works, and Jesus was simply obedient and yielded to the Father's leading. Even as everything Jesus said and did was never done independently by Him of His own accord but rather was the outgrowth of a perfect dependence upon the Father, in oneness with Him - in the same manner now, through our dependent relationship with Jesus, in oneness with Him, the Son shows us what He is doing, and we simply move together in oneness with Him, allowing Him to speak and work through us.

This is what Jesus prayed for in the upper room: *"that they all may be one, as You, Father, are in Me, and I in You; that they also may be one in Us, that the world may believe that You sent Me." (John 17:21)*. The world isn't going to believe because of all our religious activity or evangelistic strategies. They will only believe when they see and hear Him, and they will only see and hear Him when we walk in oneness with the Son, in the same manner that the Son walked in oneness with the Father.

When we simply abide in Him, walking in one yoke with Him, we will marvel as we see Christ living out His life through us. He works in us, giving us both the desire and the power to do all His good pleasure *(Phil 2:13)*. When we are truly in yoke with Him and not

111

under some burdensome legalistic or religious yoke, we will truly find rest for our souls. His yoke is easy and light because He lives and works through us while we simply abide in yoke with Him, surrendered to His will.

Many, who come into the grace movement, burned out on legalism and dead religiosity often overreact, considering any mandate to do "good works" or to "obey" to be legalism, or at best a mixed-grace message. However, if we keep in mind that all New Covenant good works are, in reality, the works of Christ in us as we simply abide in Him, being sensitive and submissive (obedient) to His every leading, then we can freely and joyfully embrace every call to obedience and good works in the New Testament. Knowing that "good works" are not referring to our own independent good works done in our own fleshly strength, but rather are the works of Christ in us; we can then enter into His rest, as seen in Hebrews:

> *"There remains therefore a rest for the people of God. 10 For **he who has entered His rest has himself also ceased from his works as God did from His**." (Heb 4:9-10)*

A group of people came to Jesus and asked Him: *"What shall we do, that we may work the works of God?" (John 6:28).* Although, there is no indication that they understood His reply, Jesus, in response, extended to them an invitation to enter into this rest of abiding faith: *"Jesus answered and said to them, 'This is the work of God that you believe in Him whom He sent."* Those who believe enter into His rest, where the works of God are done *in and through us,* not *by us,* as we simply walk in a trustful dependence upon Him, allowing Him to will and do His own good pleasure through our lives.

Genuine, Living, Active Faith, is a Gift of God's Grace

When the New Testament speaks of faith in Jesus, it is always referring to a *"trusting reliance upon"* Him, rather than a simple acknowledgment of His existence. The Greek preposition which proceeds "believe" in John 6:28 is *eis,* which would be literally translated "believe *into* Him." I prefer this literal rendering, since it clearly expresses a kind of faith which rests fully upon Jesus and cannot be easily confused with a mere mental assent.

Genuine faith, which enables us to receive Christ and continue experiencing His life lived through us, is a gift of God's grace. This can be seen in a number of passages. One worthy of mention is Ephesians 2:8:

"For by grace you have been saved through faith, and that not of yourselves; it is the gift of God" (Eph 2:8)

At the risk of being overly technical, I would like to explain why the structure of this sentence indicates that the grace-gift in this verse not only refers to our salvation, but also the very faith which appropriates it. The participle translated *"have been saved"* is masculine gender and *"faith"* is a feminine noun, whereas *"that"* is in the neuter. That would indicate that the declaration *"that not of yourselves"* is referring back to both the masculine participle *"have been saved"* and also the feminine noun *"faith."* If Paul was referring exclusively to salvation as the grace-gift without also including "faith," he would have used the masculine form of *"**that** not of yourselves"* to correspond with the masculine gender of the participle *"have been saved"* instead of the neuter. His selection of the neuter to refer to the gift, indicates that he considered both salvation and faith as being part of God's grace-gift.

Not only is *saving* faith seen as a gift of God, but we also see that our *ongoing* faith is also a gift of God's grace. A literal translation of Philippians 1:29 emphasizes that the grace-gift of faith is ongoing and not simply the faith by which we initially appropriated salvation. The Concordant Literal Version says:

*"for to you it is **graciously granted**, for Christ's sake, not only **to be believing** on Him, but to be suffering for His sake also." (Phil 1:29 CLV)*

The word translated *"graciously granted"* is the Greek word *charizomai "to give as a grace-gift,"* and is in the aorist tense. The aorist indicates that the grace-gift of faith was given at a point of time in the past. However, it was given to us not just to believe on Him, but to *continue believing* on Him, as we see expressed in the present active infinitive *"believing."* Therefore, this verse implies that the faith we have received from God will not fail but will persevere to the end.

True saving and persevering faith does not originate in man, but in God. Only those appointed to eternal life believe: *"And as many as had been appointed to eternal life believed." (Acts 13:48).* Although this is a subject for another book, mankind, before

113

regeneration, is not even able to *see* the kingdom of God, let alone believe *(John 3:3)*. We were dead in our sins until God made us alive *(Eph 2:1-10)*.

Why then doesn't God give faith to all? Why are only a chosen few given the gift of faith? Wouldn't that make God a respecter of persons? No. His election is not random. Neither is it according to human merit – it is according to grace, or the lack of human merit. God's grace is a manifestation of His loving heart, responding to the heart cry of the poor in spirit, the broken-hearted and the oppressed.

Although God loves all, His grace is selective – some receive it in this age while others don't. He doesn't extend His grace to the proud, but to the humble *(James 4:6)*. That is why Jesus said to the Pharisees: *"tax collectors and harlots enter the kingdom of God before you." (Matt 21:31)*. That is why He said that He didn't come to call the righteous but sinners to repentance *(Matt 9:13)*. God's desire is mercy, but He must withhold it from the proud and self-righteous *until* they come to see their need of grace and humble themselves to receive it. That is why not many wise, strong and noble are among the elect of this age. As Paul says:

"For you see your calling, brethren, that not many wise according to the flesh, not many mighty, not many noble, are called. 27 But **God has chosen the foolish** *things of the world to put to shame the wise, and God has chosen* **the weak** *things of the world to put to shame the things which are mighty; 28 and* **the base** *things of the world and* **the things which are despised God has chosen,** *and* **the things which are not, to bring to nothing the things that are,** *29* **that no flesh should glory in His presence.** *30 But of Him you are in Christ Jesus, who became for us wisdom from God — and righteousness and sanctification and redemption — 31 that, as it is written, 'He who glories, let him glory in the Lord."* *(1Cor 1:26-31)*

If we understand that God did not choose us based upon our merits, but rather based upon our lack thereof, all grounds of boasting are excluded. Some give glory to God for having chosen them in spite of themselves but at the same time boast that they are saved because of their own faith. The same people tend to boast of how their faith has accomplished great things. But once we recognize that we wouldn't even have faith to believe apart from grace, all grounds of boasting are excluded.

Genuine and Dynamic Faith is the "Faith of Jesus"

This leads to the question: If saving and persevering faith is not ours, but comes from above as a grace-gift from God, then whose faith is it? I believe the Scriptural answer is found in the life of the resurrected Christ who becomes our life in the new birth. Jesus Christ in us is not only the *author* of faith but also the *finisher* of faith:

*"looking unto Jesus, the **author** and **finisher** of our faith...."* (Heb 12:2)

*"looking to the **author and perfecter of faith**—Jesus...."* (Heb 12:2 Youngs Literal Translation)

We see here that Jesus is the author of faith, and also the finisher or perfecter of faith. Some translations add "our." However, the author emphasizes that the faith originates in Christ and finishes in Christ, rather than in us. For that reason, I feel that the addition of *"our"* by the translators detracts from the emphasis of the passage – that we should look unto Him and not into ourselves if we want faith that saves and perseveres to the finish line. The text actually says, *"the faith,"* not *"our faith."* Elsewhere we see that the expression *"the faith"* refers to the faith of Jesus and not our own *(Gal 3:22-25 KJV)*.

If indeed we have been crucified and raised to new life with Christ, then it is no longer we who live but it is He who lives in us. Our only righteousness is His righteousness in us. Our only wisdom is the mind of Christ within us, and our only faith is the faith of Jesus who now lives in us, just as Galatians 2:12 states in the King James Version and other older translations:

*"I am crucified with Christ: nevertheless I live; yet not I, but **Christ liveth in me**: and the life which I now live in the flesh **I live by the faith of the Son of God,** who loved me, and gave himself for me."* (Gal 2:20 KJV)

Recent scholarship has favored the rendering of *"faith of the Son,"* as an objective genitive rather than a subjective genitive. That would make the phrase say, *"faith in the Son"* instead of *"faith of the Son."* While this would favor the Arminian view, which sees salvation as depending upon *our* faith, it does not harmonize with the passages which clearly indicate that effectual faith is a gift from God and does not originate in us.

Making salvation dependent upon *our* faith, rather than the grace-gift of *His* vicarious faith, makes salvation ultimately dependent upon the will of the flesh or the will of man rather than upon the grace of God. God has chosen His elect Church, made up of the least likely candidates, in order to be displayed in the coming ages as *His* workmanship, to the praise of the glory of *His* grace in a way that will unequivocally exclude any grounds for boasting on our part. Any taint of human merit in His workmanship would detract from the praise of the glory of His grace when we are put on display to the world. I see many of the recent renderings of texts referring to the faith *of* Jesus as though it were our faith *in* Jesus, to be based more upon modern humanistic influences than upon a sound exegesis of the particular texts, as I believe a brief examination of the texts will show:

> *"But the scripture hath concluded all under sin, that **the promise by** (ek – not dia) **faith of Jesus** Christ **might be given to them that believe** (those that are believing). 23 But **before (the) faith came**, we were kept under the law, shut up unto the faith which should afterwards be revealed. 24 Wherefore the law was our schoolmaster to bring us unto Christ, that we might be justified by faith. 25 But **after that (the) faith is come**, we are no longer under a schoolmaster." (Gal 3:22-25 KJV)*

> *"But the scripture locks up all together under sin, that **the promise out of Jesus Christ's faith may be given to those who are believing**." (Gal 3:22 Concordant Literal Version)*

While some modern translations have changed *"faith **of** Jesus"* to read instead *"faith **in** Jesus,"* we see that a literal rendering of this verse militates against their interpretive rendering of the text. The promise, which comes out of the faith *of* Jesus as to its source, is given to those who are believing. In other words, if you are a believer and an heir of the promise it is because the faith of Jesus has been given to you. We have nothing in ourselves which we have not received. In this reading, all the glory goes to God where it belongs.

However, according to the New King James Version and many other modern versions, it reads: *"But the Scripture has confined all under sin that the promise **by** faith **in** Jesus Christ might be **given to those who believe**."* By mistranslating the Greek preposition *ek* as *"by"* instead of *"out of,"* rendering it to read *"faith **in** Jesus"* instead of *"faith **of** Jesus,"* they make salvation seem as though it ultimately depended upon man, rather than the grace of God and for His glory.

116

That the faith in view is Christ's faith and not man's, is even more evident in the context. In verses 23 and 25 it speaks of the time before Christ and after Christ as *"before the faith came"* and *"after the faith came."* In what sense can we say that faith didn't come until Christ? Hebrews 11 contains a long list of Old Testament saints who exercised faith before Christ came. Obviously *"the faith"* referred to in the New Covenant is not our faith but the faith of Jesus Christ, which comes to all who believe:

*"Even the righteousness of God which is **by** (dia) **faith of Jesus Christ unto all** and **upon all** them that believe (that are believing): for there is no difference." (Rom 3:22 KJV)*

*"even the righteousness of God **through the faith of Jesus Christ, toward all and upon all those who believe**. For there is no difference." (Rom 3:22 MKJV)*

Believe me, if you are believing in a saving, persevering way, it is through the faith of Jesus Christ, imparted to you by His grace. It is His faith which is imparted to you. You did not receive the righteousness of God because of *your* faith *in* Jesus which you had in and of yourself and exercised as an independent act of your own will, as some modern versions would have us believe *(see also Gal 2:16; Eph 3:11,12; Phil 3:9).*

We are Co-laborers with Christ

Some grace teachers present our role in the Christian walk as a totally passive one. Out of fear of falling into dead self-works, they are at risk of producing a passive, inert faith, void of any good works. They quote the first part of Galatians 2:20 which says: *"I have been crucified with Christ; it is no longer I who live, but Christ lives in me."* Without reading the rest of the verse, it could lead one to think that we are entirely out of the picture, but the verse doesn't stop there. Paul continues saying: *"and **the life which I now live** in the flesh **I live** by faith of the Son of God, who loved me and gave Himself for me." (Gal 2:20b)*

As those who are now one spirit with Him, we are now *in yoke* with Him – we .are co-laborers with Him. Our part is to yield to His leading, taking our directives from Him, in order that His works may be accomplished in our mortal bodies. While recognizing that Christ was now his life, Paul, instead of becoming lackadaisical and inert, labored even more, yet not he, in and of himself, but Christ in him:

*"But by the grace of God I am what I am, and **His grace toward me was not in vain; but I labored more abundantly** than they all, **yet not I, but the grace of God which was with me**." (1Cor 15:10)*

Some reason that since they are accepted by grace and Christ now lives in them, there is nothing more to do on their part. They think that if the Lord wanted to do something through them, then He would somehow take possession of their bodies and do it without any active participation on their part. But that isn't what it means to be in one yoke with the Lord.

The yoke was used to unite two oxen together. It was common for the farmer to take a strong, meek and mature ox, and put it in the same yoke with a young, undisciplined ox, so that the young ox could learn from the experienced ox how to keep going forward and how to plow a straight line. But imagine the scene if the young ox were to reason: *"I'm just going to relax and leave everything up to him. If this strong ox wants to move me, he will move me."* Then, in total dependence upon the strong mature ox, he remains passive forcing the stronger ox to drag him along, instead of moving in unison with him and learning to take his ques from him. Total passivity is not a correct understanding of the grace-walk. Total passivity, according to Paul, is receiving the grace of God in vain *(1Cor 15:10; 2Cor 6:1)*.

The apostle of grace himself, who labored more than all the rest, exhorted us to be zealous for good works more than any other apostle:

*"That you may **walk worthy of the Lord**, fully pleasing Him, **being fruitful in every good work** and increasing in the knowledge of God." (Col 1:10)*

*"Who gave Himself for us, that He might redeem us from every lawless deed and purify for Himself His own special people, **zealous for good works**." (Titus 2:14, cf. Titus 2:7; Titus 3:1; Titus 3:8; Titus 3:14; 2Tim 3:17; 2Tim 2:21; 2Thess 2:16,17; Gal 5:6; Heb 10:24; Heb 13:20,21)*

While we must guard against legalism or working for acceptance, our zeal for good works should be greater, not less, than it was under law. Works are seen as a fruit or outgrowth of Christ's life in us, but it is our responsibility to walk worthy of our calling, being fruitful in good works in a manner pleasing to the Lord. Let us take our cue from the Lord himself, who said: *"I must work the works of Him who sent Me." (John 9:4).* He said that He could do nothing apart from the Father because He only took His cues from the Father, but whatever the Father did He did in like manner. That is what it means to take Christ's yoke upon us and learn of Him.

True Living Faith Works

*"**What does it profit, my brethren, if someone says he has faith but does not have works**? **Can faith save him**? 15 If a brother or sister is naked and destitute of daily food, 16 and one of you says to them, 'Depart in peace, be warmed and filled,' but you do not give them the things which are needed for the body, what does it profit? 17 Thus also **faith by itself, if it does not have works, is dead**.*
*18 But someone will say, 'You have faith, and I have works.' Show me your faith without your works, and I will show you my faith by my works. 19 You believe that there is one God. You do well. Even the demons believe — and tremble! 20 But do you want to know, O foolish man, that faith without works is dead? 21 **Was not Abraham our father justified by works when he offered Isaac his son on the altar**? 22 **Do you see that faith was working together with his works, and by works faith was made perfect**? 23 And the Scripture was fulfilled which says, 'Abraham believed God, and it was accounted to him for righteousness.' And he was called the friend of God. 24 You see then that **a man is justified by works, and not by faith only**." (James 2:14-24)*

Most have struggled to understand what James means to say in this passage. On the surface, James here seems to be contradicting what Paul taught concerning justification by faith alone. Paul said: *"Therefore we conclude that a man is justified by faith apart from the deeds of the law." (Rom 3:28).* Here James seems to say the exact opposite: *"Thus also faith by itself, if it does not have works, is dead."* Paul used Abraham to demonstrate that we are not justified by works: *"For if Abraham was justified by works, he has something to boast about, but not before God. 3 For what does the Scripture say?*

'Abraham believed God, and it was accounted to him for righteousness." *(Rom 4:2,3).* James, on the other hand, also uses Abraham as an example, but says: *"You see then that a man is justified by works, and not by faith only."*

Martin Luther, unable to reconcile James' words with the truth of Justification by faith alone, concluded that James contradicted the rest of Scripture and therefore should not be included in the Bible. However, I believe that this seeming contradiction can be resolved when we understand that Paul and James were addressing two different audiences. Paul, presenting the gospel, emphasizes that justification is by faith alone, whereas James is confronting those who profess to already have faith, but the lack of good works in their lives indicated that they did not have the real faith – the dynamic faith – the faith of Jesus. Whereas Paul was presenting the way of salvation, James was confronting the empty profession of faith among those who claimed to be Christians but were self-deceived. Paul and James were explaining different sides of the same coin. Paul said: "faith that saves is faith alone," whereas James insists: "faith that saves is never alone."

Paul, just as James, repeatedly warned against being deluded into thinking one has saving faith when their conduct indicated otherwise. Paul said: *"Examine yourselves as to whether you are in the faith. Test yourselves. Do you not know yourselves, that Jesus Christ is in you? — unless indeed you are disqualified." (2Cor 13:5 cf.1Cor 15:2; Eph 5:3-6; 1Cor 6:9-11; Gal 5:19).* Paul also speaks of a faith that works:

*"For in Christ Jesus neither circumcision nor uncircumcision avails anything, but **faith working** through love." (Gal 5:6)*

Any grace teaching which says that since you are under grace you can do anything you want, or do nothing, if that is what you want, is not presenting the whole council of God and is turning the grace of God into licentiousness.

In what sense could we say, as James does, that we are justified by works and not by faith alone? Paul said that Abraham was justified by faith alone without works, while James says that he was justified by works when he offered up Isaac. How do we reconcile these two statements? It is important to take into account that Abraham was justified by faith *before God* the moment he believed God, and not

20 years later when he offered up Isaac. When God promised Abraham that he would have a son, it says that at that moment he was justified:

"Then He brought him outside and said, 'Look now toward heaven, and count the stars if you are able to number them.' And He said to him, 'So shall your descendants be." 6 ***And he believed in the Lord, and He accounted it to him for righteousness."*** *(Gen 15:5,6)*

On the other hand, there is no mention in Scripture that Abraham was justified when he offered up Isaac. I believe the best way to reconcile this apparent conflict is to understand that Paul is speaking from God's perspective, whereas James is speaking from man's perspective. God knows who has the true faith, justifying them by faith alone. Man, however, can only see the outward evidence of that faith, and therefore that justification is not recognized and attributed to us by others, apart from seeing some outward demonstration of it.

Paul makes it clear in Romans 4:2 that he is speaking of *justifying faith* as seen by God and not by man. James, on the other hand says: *"You say you have faith in God and have been justified? **Show me**. Give me some outward evidence of your faith and justification. What you profess may be true, but if it is true, where is the evidence?"* There is no conflict whatsoever. Paul speaks from God's perspective, just as we see in Genesis 15, whereas James speaks from man's perspective. As Jesus said: *"By their fruits you will know them." (Matt 7:20).*

Just as Abraham was justified by faith *before God*, but not until later was he seen as just *before men* when he offered up his son Isaac, thereby demonstrating that his faith was real - so also was the case with Rahab the harlot who James also presents as an example:

"Likewise, was not Rahab the harlot also justified by works when she received the messengers and sent them out another way? 26 For as the body without the spirit is dead, so faith without works is dead also." (James 2:25,26)

Rahab had heard all the stories of the deliverance of the children of Israel from Egypt; the crossing of the Red Sea; the mana from heaven and how the Lord gave them victory in battle. By the time the spies arrived in Jericho she no doubt had already believed, and in God's eyes she was already justified. But this faith and justification wasn't demonstrated for others to see until she received the spies.

This is a truth that needs to be emphasized within the grace movement. Faith that justifies and saves is faith alone, but faith that justifies is never alone. Grace teachers rightly warn of dead works done in the flesh, but they also need to warn of dead faith which doesn't result in works. Grace does not simply save and justify us – grace works.

Rewards for Good Works

*"Now if anyone builds on this foundation with gold, silver, precious stones, wood, hay, straw, 13 each one's work will become clear; for the Day will declare it, because it will be revealed by fire; and the fire will test each one's work, of what sort it is. 14 **If anyone's work which he has built on it endures, he will receive a reward**. 15 If anyone's work is burned, he will suffer loss; but he himself will be saved, yet so as through fire." (1Cor 3:12-15)*

It is common to hear grace teachers minimize or make light of any mention of us receiving rewards, a prize or treasures in heaven. They reason that, after all, they are really not our works but the works of Christ. However, as we have already seen, Christ only works through us as we yield to Him and remain in yoke with Him. Also, doing the will of the Lord often causes suffering on our part which could be averted by simply doing nothing. We have seen that it is well-pleasing to the Lord when we are fruitful in every good work. As Christians we may choose to live selfishly according to the flesh, or we may choose to die daily in order that His will, rather than ours, may be accomplished in our lives.

Many a martyr throughout the centuries has been encouraged with the expectation of heavenly rewards, yet some grace teachers actually seem to mock any such expectation. As one prominent grace teacher says:

"In reality, the term rewards does not appear anywhere in the New Testament. The apostle Paul speaks of a 'reward' (singular, not plural) or a 'prize' in the context of running a race and reaching the end. But Paul also notes that everything else is like garbage next to knowing Christ Jesus (Philippians 3: 8). Given this truth,

do we really believe that God will be awarding larger homes and nicer jewelry to those who depended on Jesus more?... But doesn't Jesus himself tell us to store up treasures in heaven (Matthew 6: 20)? Yes, but treasures aren't rewards. People discover treasures. They don't earn them." [12]

I doubt very much that the Christian martyrs were motivated to keep the faith in hopes of jewelry or a larger home in heaven. Without a doubt their life's motivation, just as with Paul, was to know Jesus Christ and to be well-pleasing to the Father. But didn't Paul himself encourage us to run so as to win?

*"Do you not know that those who run in a race all run, but one receives **the prize? Run in such a way that you may obtain it.** 25 And everyone who **competes for the prize** is temperate in all things. Now they do it to obtain a perishable crown, but we for an imperishable crown." (1Cor 9:24,25)*

The crown in view here is not a royal golden crown with jewels, but rather a wreath (*stephanos* – "wreath"), such as those given to the Olympic contestants who performed well, as a reward. He says that while the Olympic wreath is perishable, our heavenly reward is imperishable. Peter also speaks of the *unfadable* crown *(stephanos)* which will be given to all faithful pastors when Christ appears:

"And when the Chief Shepherd appears, you will receive the crown of glory that does not fade away." (1Peter 5:4)

Paul, speaking along the same line, says of the believers in Thessalonica that they were his reward at Christ's coming:

*"For what is our hope, or joy, or **crown** (stephanos) of rejoicing? Is it not even you in the presence of our Lord Jesus Christ **at His coming**? 20 For you are our glory and joy." (1Thess 2:19-20)*

Here we see that the souls of those whom we have shared the gospel with and discipled in this life will be an eternal crown of glory for us. To imply that it is unspiritual to aspire to receive the Lord's well done in anticipation of a reward, is to also imply that Paul, Peter

---

[12] Farley, Andrew; Farley, Andrew. The Naked Gospel: Truth You May Never Hear in Church (p. 168, 170). Zondervan. Kindle Edition.

and multitudes of saints who persevered, were also unspiritual. It even implies that Jesus Himself was unspiritual, since He also ran for the prize:

*"Therefore we also, since we are surrounded by so great a cloud of witnesses, let us lay aside every weight, and the sin which so easily ensnares us, and let us run with endurance the race that is set before us, 2 looking unto Jesus, the author and finisher of our faith, who **for the joy that was set before Him endured the cross, despising the shame, and has sat down at the right hand of the throne of God.**" (Heb 12:1,2)*

Jesus was clearly referring to rewards in heaven when He said that we should lay up for ourselves treasures in heaven. Contrary to what the above author says, the heavenly treasures are not buried for us in heaven, so as to need to be dug up and discovered. They are laid up by us in the heavenly treasury as we invest in the spiritual, rather than the earthly and carnal.

Also, Jesus said that suffering for Him has a great reward:

*"Blessed are you when they revile and persecute you, and say all kinds of evil against you falsely for My sake. 12 Rejoice and be exceedingly glad, **for great is your reward in heaven,** for so they persecuted the prophets who were before you."* (Matt 5:11-12)

He also said to the Church: *"Be faithful until death, and I will give you the crown (stehpanos) of life."* (Rev 2:10). Paul also says that rewards await those who suffer for His name: *"For our light affliction, which is but for a moment, is working for us a far more exceeding and eternal weight of glory."* (2Cor 4:17). To say that the word "rewards" never appears in plural form is immaterial. The fact remains that, one way or another, everything we suffer for His name's sake, and everything we do in this life in yoke with Christ and for the kingdom of God, will have an exceedingly great reward.

As believers, we will never again be condemned for our sins. We will not be judged at the Great White Throne *(thronos)* Judgment because we have already been justified and perfected forever through Christ's once and for all sacrifice for sins *(John 5:24)*. The only judgment seat we will stand before is the Bema Seat of Christ:

"For we must all appear before the judgment seat (bema) of Christ, that each one may receive the things done in the body, according to what he has done, whether good or bad." (2Cor 5:10)

Notice that two different Greek words are used for the judge's throne. The White Throne Judgment that is judicial is *thronos,* but the word for the Judgment Seat of Christ is *bema*, which is the same word used of the seats of the judges at the Olympics. The Olympic judges weighed the good moves against the errors committed by the contestants and meted out rewards in the form of wreaths *(stephanos)* to those who competed well. There is no condemnation for those who are in Christ Jesus, but there is a Bema judgment to determine what rewards will be granted or lost.

Also, our sins are not brought up in this judgment, but rather our works are judged in order to see whether they were good and beneficial, or trivial and worthless. The words *"good or bad"* used in 2Corinthians 5:10 are not the words normally used to express that which is morally good or evil, but rather that which is useful or worthless. The word *"good"* is *agathos,* which usually means *"good or beneficial."* The word *"bad"* is neither *kakos* nor *poneros* which mean *"morally bad or evil,"* but rather *faulos*, meaning *"bad in the sense of trivial or worthless."* [13] From this Greek word we derive the term *"foul ball."*

Paul is referring to the same judgment in 1Corinthians when he speaks of the day when all we have done, rather good or useless, will pass through fire and we will be rewarded for all that survives His consuming fire:

"For no other foundation can anyone lay than that which is laid, which is Jesus Christ. 12 Now if anyone builds on this foundation with gold, silver, precious stones, wood, hay, straw, 13 **each one's work will become clear;** *for the Day will declare it, because it will be revealed by fire; and* **the fire will test each one's work, of what sort it is.** *14 If anyone's work which he has built on it endures,* **he will receive a reward.** *15 If anyone's work is burned, he will suffer loss;* **but he himself will be saved,** *yet so as through fire." (1Cor 3:11-15)*

---

[13] from Vine's Expository Dictionary of Biblical Words, Copyright © 1985, Thomas Nelson Publishers.

In this judgment our salvation is not in question. That was already settled at the Cross. Here, our works are examined to see if they are good or worthless, and we will be rewarded for every good work. This is not works salvation, it is Christ giving out rewards as promised to those who have suffered for His name and invested their lives in the kingdom of God. The purpose and end result of this Bema Judgment is that the Lord may commend us for the good we have done. Paul says of this judgment:

> *"For I know of nothing against myself, yet I am not justified by this; but He who judges me is the Lord. 5 Therefore judge nothing before the time, until the Lord comes, who will both bring to light the hidden things of darkness and reveal the counsels of the hearts. **Then each one's praise will come from God**." (1Cor 4:4-5)*

What amazing grace! The only judgment God's justified children will face at Christ's coming is when He examines our earthly lives in order to praise us for what we have suffered for the cause of Christ and done for His kingdom in this life.

Chapter seven

Living out Our New Reality

As we have seen, our inner core is a brand-new creation, having been recreated in Christ, perfect in true righteousness and holiness. Our spirits are inseparably united with the Lord Jesus Christ through the new birth. We are now co-heirs with Him; His perfect righteousness is our righteousness; His authority is our authority; His mind is our mind.

The question immediately arises: If all this is true, then why do we see such a lack of holiness, authority and discernment within the Church today? Why isn't the life of Christ being lived out in the lives of so many Christians? We have already seen that God is faithful from His side and has promised that after we have suffered a little while He will Himself perfect, establish, strengthen, and settle us *(1Peter 5:10)*. He, in His unfailing commitment to our growth, delivers us over to death in order that the life of Christ in us may be manifest through our mortal bodies.

It should be obvious that, although God's timeframe varies with each of His children according to their makeup and His distinct purpose for each individual, many continue to be carnal and self-centered, even after decades have passed, in spite of the Father's faithful, consistent discipline. Even after many years their spirit remains trapped within a body which is dominated by the desires of their own flesh. They are still soulish, having the mind of the flesh, rather than the mind of Christ. The Father has a process for each of us that requires time. We cannot shorten that time, but it is apparent that many, for one reason or another, have prolonged the process. In these two final chapters we will consider some of the reasons why this process may be unnecessarily delayed in the lives of some of His children.

Obedience Required

*"**As obedient children**, not conforming yourselves to the former lusts, as in your ignorance; 15 but as He who called you is holy, you also be holy in all your conduct, 16 because it is written, 'Be holy, for I am holy.' 17 And if you call on the Father, who without*

partiality judges according to each one's work, conduct yourselves throughout the time of your stay here in fear." (1Peter 1:14-17)

If you have been born again you are God's child and He will never "un-child" you. He will discipline you and even *scourge* you when necessary, but upon receiving His life, He takes responsibility for your formation, bringing you up into the image of Christ.

However, as any parent who has more than one child knows, not all children respond equally to paternal discipline. Even when the father is impartial in applying the same standard to all his children, one child will often be more inclined to rebel against his authority as father, whereas another child may be submissive and teachable. The submissive child, submitting himself to the father's authority, requires little corrective intervention and matures rapidly, whereas the rebellious child often passes into adulthood without ever maturing, in spite of the father's faithful, consistent corrections.

Peter, in the above passage carries this analogy over into our relationship to God as our Father. Our heavenly Father is impartial and loves us all equally, but some of His children are more obstinate and disobedient than others, despising His authority over them because it conflicts with their own self-will. These obstinate, rebellious children are those most inclined to reject the reproofs of Scripture, seeking out teachers who will tell them they are okay just as they are, even though they are in rebellion against God. This is especially true of our generation in which parental discipline has been despised and rejected by society. That is why Paul said of our time:

*"Preach the word! Be ready in season and out of season. Convince, rebuke, exhort, with all longsuffering and teaching. 3 For **the time will come when they will not endure sound doctrine, but according to their own desires, because they have itching ears, they will heap up for themselves teachers**; 4 and they will turn their ears away from the truth, and be turned aside to fables." (2Tim 4:2-4)*

Sadly, much of what passes as grace teaching today, fulfills this prophecy to the letter. Many disobedient children in this generation, in their rebellion against God's Word and His rightful authority over their lives, are seeking out teachers who teach a false version of grace which caters to their own rebellious self-will. Such believers (if indeed they are believers), must repent and align their lives to the Word of God, submitting to His paternal authority over them. Otherwise, they will never mature into the image of Christ, and all they will have to show for their lives on earth will be wood, hay and stubble. Paul was speaking to us as God's children when he warned: *"Do not be deceived, God is not mocked; for whatever a man sows, that he will also reap." (Gal 6:7).*

The obedience spoken of here is our obedience as children of God. It is obedience *from* acceptance - not obedience *for* acceptance. Even Jesus, being sinless, was brought to perfection or maturity by obedience to the Father in the midst of suffering and opposition: *"though He was a Son, yet He learned obedience by the things which He suffered. 9 And having been perfected, He became the author of eternal salvation to all who obey Him." (Heb 5:8,9).* We, in like manner, have been called to a life of obedience to the Father in union with the Son.

If just hearing the New Testament commands to obey causes something within you to rise up in rebellion against any claim to authority over your life, instead of rejecting the call to submit, embrace it, receiving grace from the Father, which will enable you to walk as His obedient child in loving submission to Him:

"Therefore humble yourselves under the mighty hand of God, that He may exalt you in due time, 7 casting all your care upon Him, for He cares for you." (1Peter 5:6-7)

A word of warning is needed for those who remain in the valley of decision – undecided whether to obey God or seek after teachers who cater to their own rebellious self-will. Be persuaded by the truth of God's Word rather than allowing yourself to be swayed by some supernatural sign or wonder alone. Jesus warned that a wicked and adulterous generation seeks after a sign *(Matt 16:4).* Although Jesus performed many signs and wonders and promised that greater signs would follow those who believe on Him, our faith should be built upon His truth, and not upon the mere presence of the supernatural.

We are called to love and serve a supernatural God and should believe Him for miracles, signs and wonders, but if we do not embrace His truth, preferring rather to have our ears tickled with a false version of grace which requires no commitment on our part, we put ourselves in danger of believing the lie. As Paul once again warns concerning the final deception:

*"The coming of the lawless one is according to the working of Satan, **with all power, signs, and lying wonders**, 10 and with all **unrighteous deception** among those who perish, because **they did not receive the love of the truth, that they might be saved**. 11 And for this reason God will send them strong delusion, that they should believe the lie, 12 that they all may be condemned **who did not believe the truth but had pleasure in unrighteousness**." (2Thess 2:9-12)*

While Paul makes it clear that he is talking here of unbelievers who will believe the lie and be condemned, Jesus warned that the final deception would be so great that it would deceive, if possible, the very elect of God *(Matt 24:24)*. While there is a growing movement within the modern-day Church which teaches that none of these warnings apply to us today, having been fulfilled prior to the destruction of Jerusalem in A.D. 70, that doctrine is, in and of itself, a part of the end-time deception. (see my book *"Last Days – Past or Present?"*, Amazon, kindle edition).

There is a common saying: *"If the shoe fits, wear it."* If your love of sin and unrighteousness is greater than your love for God and His truth, you need to examine your calling and election to determine whether or not you are really in the faith *(2Peter 1:10)*. However, if after being weighed in the balance you are found wanting, don't despair, because His arms are open wide to receive all who repent of their sin and rebellion, and receive Christ. If you see your need and receive Him, it is because the Father has drawn you, and the good work which He begins in your life He will perfect.

Some readers, who were simply looking for another book on grace, may have stopped reading the moment I mentioned obedience. However, this book is about the true grace of God, and the true grace of God results in one being transformed into Christ's own likeness. It receives us where we are, but will never leave us where we are, but will take us from glory to glory, as we walk in loving submission to Him.

Transformation through the Renewal of Our Mind

*"And do not be conformed to this world, but **be transformed by the renewing of your mind**, that you may prove what is that good and acceptable and perfect will of God." (Rom 12:2)*

Having considered the problem of outright, self-willed rebellion in the hearts of some of God's disobedient children, it is nevertheless probably correct to say that the vast majority of those who do not experience freedom and transformation are not willfully rebellious. When a born again child of God walks in willful rebellion (as we all have sadly done on occasions), they are acting contrary to who they now are in their innermost being. Even while they are acting in disobedience, the indwelling Holy Spirit grieves within them, and they do so against the inner desires of their new, perfect spirit.

Most of us earnestly desire to walk in obedience, just as Paul in Romans 7. But try as they may, many continue to struggle with defeat and bondage to the power of indwelling sin. As Paul learned in his Romans 7 struggle, the flesh is of no profit when it comes to being transformed into the image of Christ:

"For I know that in me (that is, in my flesh) nothing good dwells; for to will is present with me, but how to perform what is good I do not find. 19 For the good that I will to do, I do not do; but the evil I will not to do, that I practice." (Rom 7:18,19)

The flesh is hopelessly incorrigible and incapable of submitting to God *(Rom 8:7,8)*. At best, it can only pride itself in an outward appearance of conformity to God's law. But any holiness we may attain to by self-effort is dead works and not the holiness of Christ, who is now our life.

Many fail to understand that the Christian walk is nothing other than Christ living in us. Anything outside of that is at best a fleshly conformation to a false caricature of true holiness. In Christ, we are called to a *transformation* into Christ's likeness, not a *conformation* to some external standard of holiness. That is what Jesus was saying when He said in Matthew 5:20: *"unless your righteousness exceeds the righteousness of the scribes and Pharisees, you will by no means enter the kingdom of heaven."* The word here translated *"exceed"* is *perisseuo*, which Strong's defines as *"to superabound (in quantity or quality)."*

Obviously, Jesus wasn't referring to the quantity of rules one keeps, since He reproached the Pharisees on numerous occasions for their excesses in observing additional commandments of men, such as the washing of hands and their meticulous tithing, down to such minutiae as giving a tenth of their household spices like mint, anise and cumin *(Matt 23:23)*. Jesus was not speaking of a *quantitatively* greater standard of righteousness, but rather was speaking of a different *quality* of righteousness - the righteousness which would be imputed and imparted to those who believe in Him. The same word *perisseuo* is used to refer to the superabundant grace and the gift of His righteousness, which is graciously given to us, causing us to reign in life through Him *(Rom 5:15-17)*.

Paul explains that the transformation which every child of God inwardly longs for comes through the renewing of our minds *(Rom 12:2)*. Transformation is not achieved through *right doing* but rather through *right believing*, and in order to believe right we must be renewed in our mind. Faith comes by hearing the truth concerning Christ:

"So faith comes from hearing, and hearing by the word of Christ." (Rom 10:17 NASU)

It is important to note that the older Greek manuscripts say that faith comes by hearing *"the word of Christ,"* rather than *"the word of God."* Accordingly, most recent translations render it *"the word of Christ."* It is *the word of Christ* that saves and transforms us. We have already seen that, although all Scripture is inspired of God and profitable for the purpose for which it was given to us, not all Scripture imparts saving, transforming faith. The law, although it was given to lead us to faith, produces self-despair rather than faith. It drives us to despair of self, in order that we might afterwards have ears to hear the good news concerning the word of Christ.

The word concerning Christ is the central theme of Scripture, from the promised seed of Eve in Genesis 3:15, to the Jewish sacrificial system which pointed to His redemptive work on the cross, to the open invitation of *"whosoever will"* in the last chapter of Revelation. He is the Alpha and the Omega, First and the Last, the Beginning and the End *(Rev 22:13)*.

Whereas the Law condemns, *the word of Christ* produces faith and hope. Where the Law kills, the gospel of Christ imparts new life. Without minimizing the importance of knowing the Law, it is the word of Christ we are to focus upon. The Pharisees had the words of the

Law, but the Law does not give life. When Jesus asked the disciples if they wished to continue following Him, Peter replied: *"Lord, to whom shall we go? You have the words of eternal life." (John 6:68).* That is why we are exhorted by Paul to let *the word of Christ* dwell richly in us *(Col 3:16).*

Our new identity and life is *Christ in us.* Therefore, our transformation comes through knowing, believing and walking according to the truth of who we now are in Him:

> *"But you have not so **learned Christ**, 21 if indeed you have heard Him and have been **taught by Him**, **as the truth is in Jesus**: 22 that **you put off** (aorist - "once and for all"), concerning your former conduct, the old man which grows corrupt according to the deceitful lusts, 23 and be renewed in the spirit of your mind, 24 and that **you put on** (aorist – "once and for all") the new man which **was created** (aorist – "once and for all") according to God, in true righteousness and holiness." (Eph 4:20-24)* [14]

Living in the New Reality of who we now are in Christ

---

[14] Both *"you put off"* and *"you put on"* are aorist, middle, infinitive verbs. Aorist, when used in a verb other than indicative mood does not necessarily speak of the time of action but rather to the kind of action. The aorist tense speaks of a once for all action. That is why the Greek scholar Kenneth Wuest reads Ephesians 4:24 as follows in his *Expanded New Testament:* *"But as for you, not in this manner did you learn the Christ, since, indeed, as is the case, you heard and in Him were taught just as truth is in Jesus, that **you have put off once for all** with reference to your former manner of life the old self who is being corrupted according to the passionate desires of deceit; moreover, that you are being constantly renewed with reference to the spirit of your mind; and that **you have put on once for all** the new self who after God was created in righteousness and holiness of truth."* *(from The New Testament: An Expanded Translation by Kenneth S. Wuest Copyright © 1961 by Wm. B. Eerdmans Publishing Co.)* Some translations actually translate it as imperative *"put on"* and *"put off."* However, such a rendering is not only uncommon for the infinitive form of the verb, but also goes against the truth in Jesus as revealed in other texts. *(Rom 6:1-4; Col 3:9,10)* It presents the truth in Jesus as if it were *what we do* rather than *what we already are in Christ.*

Most Christians do not experience transformation simply because they have not learned the truth concerning who they now are in Christ. In their ignorance of the truth as it is in Jesus, they are actually trying to become what they already are. In the passage we just saw in Ephesians 4, Paul is not speaking about something we must do, but rather he is telling us what already took place when we believed in Jesus. He is not commanding us to put off the old man and put on the new – he is informing us concerning the truth as it is in Jesus – the truth that we, in the past, already put off the old man, and that having put on the new man, we are now an entirely new creation in Christ. As we learn Christ, being renewed in the spirit of our mind, we begin to live according to who we now truly are in Him.

Many think that when they stop sinning they are putting off the old man, which they understand to be their "old nature." However, the reality is that the old man is no longer us. We have been created anew in Christ: we are now a new man in Him. Before, as the old man in Adam, sin was normal for us. But now we are an entirely new man in Christ. The old man was crucified and done away with *(Rom 6:6)*. We don't stop sinning to become new – we stop sinning because we already are a new man in Christ:

> *"Do not lie to one another, **since** you **have put off** (aorist – "once and for all") the old man with his deeds, 10 and **have put on** (aorist – "once and for all") the new man who is **renewed in knowledge** according to the image of Him who **created** him (aorist – "once and for all")." (Col 3:9-10)*

Sin in the life of a believer is a mental problem – it does not stem from a supposed "old nature" within us. Our old man is already dead and gone forever. We sin due to lack of knowledge of who we really are in Christ. A believer who struggles with the ghost of the old man, suffers from spiritual amnesia. He has forgotten, or does not understand, that his old man already died, and his new man has already been created in true righteousness and holiness. That is why Paul says that we need to *awake to righteousness (1Cor 15:34)*. True righteousness is not something to be achieved but something we already have in Christ, and we simply need to be awakened to it in order to stop sinning. We need to be *renewed in knowledge or renewed in the spirit of our mind*. Our real problem is not that the old man is still with us, but rather that we think it is, and act accordingly.

Paul, in Romans six, reproaches those who think grace leads to more sin. He tells them that their problem is in their mind. He says:

"Don't you know?" "Don't you know that you died with Christ to the old man and arose with Him to newness of life?" Once we really understand and believe that our old man died, and we are a new man in Christ, we will begin to experience freedom from sin, and the Christ-life being lived out in our mortal bodies.

Know, Reckon and Yield

Romans six is divided in three parts, 1) *Know* 2) *Reckon* and 3) *Yield*. The first ten verses summarize what we need to *know*. Transformation begins with the renewing of our minds, when we learn the truth as it is in Christ. We need to know that we have died to the old man, and that through our union with Christ in our spirit, we are now a new man – a new creation altogether.

However, knowledge, in and of itself, does not produce transformation. We need to *reckon* it to be true. In verse eleven Paul follows up by saying:

*"Likewise you also, __reckon__ yourselves to be **dead indeed to sin,** but **alive to God in Christ** Jesus our Lord." (Rom 6:11)*

Reckoning is where the truth dawns upon us and our knowledge becomes wedded to our faith. To illustrate this, imagine that the bank was to send you a letter informing you that a wealthy man had deposited a million dollars into your account. Your first reaction would probably be *"it's too good to be true."* Many who hear the gospel of grace don't benefit from it because they reason that it is just too good to be true.

Maybe you decide to ask your friends what they think about the letter from the bank, and they look at it and say: *"I know that it seems to say that you were given one million dollars as a gift, but nothing is free in this life." "What the letter is really saying is that the gentleman is giving you a line of credit for one million dollars. But if you take the money out of the bank and spend it, then you will end up having to pay it all back with interest."*

Many, skeptical of free grace, will rob you of the truth by telling you that the word of Christ doesn't really mean what it seems to mean. If you allow them to convince you, you will continue to struggle along and never benefit from your new reality in Christ, even though it is indeed the truth. Even though you really do have a free gift of one million dollars in your bank account, if you don't reckon it to be true and begin to live according to the new reality that you are now a millionaire, you will have received the gift in vain.

When we truly reckon or consider ourselves to be dead indeed to sin and alive in Christ, we can then begin to live according to the new reality of who we now are in Christ, yielding or presenting ourselves to God as who we now truly are - instruments of righteousness:

> *"Therefore do not let sin reign in your mortal body, that you should obey it in its lusts. 13 And do not present your members as instruments of unrighteousness to sin, but* **present yourselves to God as being alive from the dead, and your members as instruments of righteousness to God**. *14 For sin shall not have dominion over you, for you are not under law but under grace."* *(Rom 6:12-14)*

Jesus said: *"you shall know the truth, and the truth shall make you free."* Right believing leads to right living. Transformation only comes through being renewed in the spirit of our minds, through the knowledge of our new identity in Christ. We are not to be conformed to this world but transformed by the renewing of our minds according to the mind of Christ.

In our perfect, born again spirit we already have the mind of Christ, but our soul needs to be renewed. This renewal does not commence with our emotions or with our will, but rather in our minds. *"As a man* ***thinks*** *in his heart, so is he." (Pr 23:7).* If your mind is programmed to believe according to the world, you are going to act like the world. On the other hand, if you allow your mind to be renewed, letting the word of Christ dwell richly in you, He will take you from faith to faith, from glory to glory. Let us not conform ourselves to the mindset of this world, whether it be religious or secular, but rather *"receive with meekness the implanted word, which is able to save your souls." (James 1:21).*

Chapter eight

The Battle for the Mind

*"For though we walk in the flesh, we do not war according to the flesh. 4 For the weapons of our warfare are not carnal but mighty in God for pulling down strongholds, 5 **casting down arguments and every high thing that exalts itself against the knowledge of God, bringing every thought into captivity to the obedience of Christ.**" (2Cor 10:3-5)*

The passage above is often quoted in the context of spiritual warfare, especially in reference to tearing down the strongholds of the enemy in our cities and our nation. Without minimizing its application to spiritual warfare in our cities and nations, it should be pointed out that Paul, in the context, is speaking of strongholds against the knowledge of God which the enemy builds in our minds – in our own personal thought-life. Even as Jesus fought His greatest battle at a place called *"The Place of the Skull,"* our greatest battle is fought in the place of the skull - the *mind.*

Satan, the god of this age, is battling for our minds because he knows that as a man thinks in his heart, so is he. This world system is satanic and antichrist. Even though it is often cloaked in the form of benevolence, tolerance, humanitarianism and science, it always exalts self against the knowledge of God and a humble dependence upon Christ. Especially in this age of information, through media and entertainment, our minds are being programmed by the mastermind behind it – the devil. From infancy we are programmed to focus upon self and humanity, to the exclusion of God.

When we come to Christ, we receive the mind of Christ in our new spirit, but *our* mind, which is of the soul, still has a lifetime of the enemy's strongholds which keep us from living according to the truth as it is in Jesus. They need to be torn down before we can experience transformation in our soul. In multiple ways the world has been an effective tool of the enemy of our souls to build strong fortresses in our thought-life, thereby taking our will and emotions captive. In this manner he keeps us from really knowing God as He is, and from being subject to Christ in our hearts.

However, God has not left us defenseless. In this battle for the mind, He has given us powerful weapons which, when properly used, will demolish completely all the enemy's fortresses in our minds and hearts. As we learn the truth as it is in Christ, that truth will set us free as we are renewed in our minds, according to our new reality in Him, rather than continuing in bondage to the thought patterns of the old man.

The strongholds of the enemy either consist of lies, the distortion of the truth, or the perpetuation of beliefs according to our former reality in Adam which are no longer true of us now that we are a new creation in Christ. It is knowing the truth and activating it by faith that will set us free.

Confronting the Enemy's Lies with the Truth

As we learn the truth as it is in Christ and believe it in our heart and begin to confess it with our mouth, the lies that have fettered and tormented us will lose their grip upon our minds and hearts, and we will begin to enjoy a new intimacy and freedom from the power of indwelling sin. Right living begins with right believing. As long as our beliefs are wrong no other discipline will be of any avail against the strongholds of the enemy in our lives.

The following are some of the lies which have been sown in our hearts which must be confronted and replaced with the truth. Since these false beliefs are so commonly held and defended in the religious world, and we have believed them all our lives, they have become deeply rooted in our souls. They are arguments constructed by the enemy which must be cast down by bringing every thought captive to the obedience to the glorious gospel of Jesus Christ. Only a revelation of the truth of the gospel, written upon our hearts, can uproot these strongholds, and set us free to obey Christ.

Lie: God is Love, But...

The most basic need of man is to be loved. When someone loses all hope of ever being loved, life becomes unbearable for that person, and if he doesn't actually take his life, it will simply waste away from the inside out. The need for love is innate in all rational creatures. Why is this so? We find the answer in the Scriptures, which declare that God is love *(1John 4:8)*. We also see in Scripture that all creation finds its origin in God:

> *"For of (ek) Him and through (dia) Him and to (eis) Him are all things, to whom be glory forever. Amen." (Rom 11:36)*

Theologians since Augustine would have us believe that God simply made us out of nothing *(ex nihilo)*, but the Scriptures reveal something much more meaningful than that. Instead of coming into existence out of nothing *(ex nihilo)*, we find that our origin is in God *("out of God" Lat. "ex Deus", Gr. "ek theos")*. Although creation at present has lost its way and has been subjected to vanity, we were made by Love and for Love and therefore we cannot bear to exist without at least the hope of being loved unconditionally and without some sense that our lives have significant meaning and purpose for someone.

The world's Christianity deprives man of both the sense of personal worth and the unconditional love of our Creator. As to man's worth before God and His love for us even at our worst, we only need to look at the cross and see the Father in Christ, reconciling us back to Himself *(2Cor 5:19)*. We often hear pious refrains like: *"You need God, He doesn't need you."* While this saying may be true of God in an existential sense, it fails miserably in revealing Father God's heart towards His wayward children. When we hear a betrayed husband say to his unfaithful wife: *"I don't need you,"* we know that his heart is really broken and that his words are simply a form of self-defense. However, unlike sinful man, the Father's love does not say: *"I don't need you."* On the contrary, His love goes out to us even in the midst of our rebellion, saying things like:

> *"**How can I give you up**, Ephraim? How can I hand you over, Israel? How can I make you like Admah? How can I set you like Zeboiim? **My heart churns within Me; My sympathy is stirred**. 9 **I will not execute the fierceness of My anger**; I will not again destroy Ephraim. **For I am God, and not man, The Holy One** in your midst; And I will not come with terror." (Hos 11:8-9)*

In Hosea we see that God's people were unfaithful to Him even though He was a husband to them. Nevertheless, He continued being faithful to them. Those who really know the heart of God like Jeremiah, can say even in the midst of His fierce judgments:

*"For **the Lord will not cast off forever**. 32 Though He causes grief, yet He will show compassion according to the multitude of His mercies. 33 For **He does not afflict willingly**, nor grieve the children of men." (Lam 3:31-33)*

*"The Lord is merciful and gracious; slow to anger, and **abounding in mercy**. 9 He will not always strive with us, **nor will He keep His anger forever**." (Ps 103:8-9)*

However, since Augustine changed the face of God in the fifth century, God's love has been limited or even redefined by a little three letter word: "**but**…" *"God is love, **but** He is also wrath." "God is love, **but** if you don't respond to His love soon enough, He will hate you and torture you forever." "God is love, **but** He is also hate and He hates all sinners except for the elect."* They say: *"God is love, **but** He is also holy."* But since when is love separable from holiness? Is God divisible? No. Love fulfills all righteousness. Therefore, love is holiness, and holiness is love. Holiness apart from love is not true holiness, but mere heartless Phariseeism. Holiness without love is what crucified our Lord.

They say that God is love but, because He is holy, He must punish with eternal wrath. However, in the verses cited above we see that it is precisely because He is The Holy One, that he will not execute the fullness of His wrath. It is because of His love/holiness that He Himself made reconciliation for all through the blood of His cross *(Col 1:20)*. Now God can be just and at the same time the justifier of the ungodly when they receive Jesus *(Rom 3:26)*.

Instead of seeing God's judgments, anger, wrath, and discipline as manifestations or attributes of God's paternal love, they attempt to divide God's personality. They say that God is love, but He is also hate; He is love, but He is also wrath, etc. However, the Bible doesn't simply say that God loves, but that He *is* love. That is His essence, or who He is. The same could not be said of the other attributes or manifestations of God's character. God hates, but He is not hate. God gets angry, but He is not anger. God even rejects, but not forever because God is love and not hate or rejection *(Lam 3:31-33; Ps 103:8-9)*.

There is not enough space in this book to adequately deal with all the ramifications of the enemy's stronghold of *"God is love, **but**…"* What little I have said here has probably only served to stir up this mental stronghold for some. This subject is treated in greater detail in my book *"The Triumph of Mercy."* [15] Nevertheless, it is a major stronghold of the enemy that needs to be confronted. Those who believe that God's nature is divided, and love is conditional, live in constant fear that God does not really love them, or that His love for them may end. They end up living most of their lives on the other side of *"**but**,"* instead of feeling secure in His love.

Lie: God loves you if...

Many of those who manage to get past religions' *"buts"* that limit God's love, still do not feel secure in God's love because of the *"ifs."* *"God loves you **if**..."* *"God will love you **as long as**..."* Most Christians struggle with the love of God. One moment they feel that God loves them and the next moment they doubt He loves them. The reason is because they are taught two irreconcilable statements concerning God's love: 1) God's love is unconditional and 2) God's love is conditional. Both cannot be true, but traditional theology would have us believe that they are, and for that reason, many Christians live in a quandary, never certain which of the two is true for them in any given moment. Most live the greater part of their lives believing in their heart that God's love is conditional, because it is the kind of love that they have been most acquainted with since infancy.

In spite of the fact that the Bible declares that God is love, most do not believe in their heart of hearts that His love is unfailing and that He loves them unconditionally. Due to a lifetime of experiencing conditional love and being taught doctrines that communicate to us that, although He loves, He cannot really *be* love, most live in constant fear of His disapproval or rejection. Their sense of security is based upon their own works and performance rather than resting in the love and grace of God. When they perform well, they feel moments of acceptance, but no matter how much we do, the accuser is always telling us that we haven't done enough.

We all need to comprehend the father-heart of God. Although Jesus said that we, as earthly fathers, are evil fathers by comparison, very few of us would ever stop loving our child just because he falls short of our expectations. We may become very angry with them

---

[15] *The Triumph of Mercy*, George Hurd. Kindle edition.

(wrath), and even discipline them (judgment), but the very motive behind our anger and discipline is our unfailing love for our disobedient child. The absence of anger and corrective discipline is not an indication of love but rather the absence of love. The Scriptures tell us that God's severity is an evidence of His love, not His rejection or abandonment:

*"For whom the Lord **loves** He chastens, and **scourges** every son whom He receives." (Heb 12:6)*

These are some pretty strong words. It is the same terminology as used of the unfaithful servant who receives many stripes (a scourging) when his master returns *(Luke 12:46-48).* The word *"scourge" (Gr. mastao)* is the same word used of the Roman scourging of Jesus, yet we see here that, when necessary, the Father scourges us, but when He does it is because He loves us. Even His anger and wrath does not last forever because, although God gets angry and even casts some away for a time, it is not forever because God is love *(1John 4:8; Lam 3:31-33; Ps 103:8-9).*

Unconditional love does not mean that God just smiles at us when we willfully disobey. Unconditional love means that even when He afflicts us, His love for us never ceases and His mercies never come to an end. Once we understand that Father God's love is unconditional, no matter what, this stronghold in our mind and heart is demolished. Then we can confidently draw near to the Father and receive of His fullness, which alone brings transformation.

We also need to understand that the enemy is not ignorant of the Scriptures and he is an expert at taking verses out of context and using them against us, just as he did in the temptation of Jesus. Bible verses are some of his favorite weapons. One of the texts He takes out of context in order to cause us to doubt God's unconditional love, is the words of Jesus in John 14:23:

"If anyone loves Me, he will keep My word; and My Father will love him, and We will come to him and make Our home with him." (John 14:23)

This verse, taken by itself, has led some to think that God's love is conditional. However, one must keep in mind what John said earlier in John 3:16 *"For God so loved **the world** that He gave His only begotten Son..."* Even while we were enemies God loved us and sent His Son to give His life for us *(Rom 5:10)*. Did the father of the prodigal son stop loving his son when he left home? No. The Father's love is constant. Then what does Jesus mean when He says that the Father loves and abides with his obedient sons? In the same way that the Lord is present everywhere all the time, and yet He manifests Himself in a special way when two or three are gathered in His name, God's relationship is more intimate with those who abide in Him, than with the rebellious wayward child.

James says: *"Draw near to God and He will draw near to you."* *(James 4:8)*. There is some truth to the saying, *"If you feel far from God, guess who moved."* Three verses earlier James said to the worldly among them: *"Do you think that the Scripture says in vain, 'The Spirit who dwells in us yearns jealously?" (James 4:5)*. God doesn't stop loving us when we are worldly; His love simply manifests in a different manner – that of jealous yearning for our hearts. When, in 1John 2:15, it says, *"If anyone loves the world, the love of the Father is not in him,"* it doesn't mean that the Father stops loving us but rather that when we love the world we are not abiding in His love, and instead of being in communion with Him, He is - relationally speaking, at a distance, jealously yearning for our hearts to turn back to Him.

If you do not feel secure in the love of God at all times, then you need to learn the truth as it is in Jesus. You need to be renewed in the spirit of your mind so as to be made perfect in love, because perfect love casts out the stronghold of fear – not *your* perfect love, but a comprehension of *His* perfect love for you which never ceases *(1John 4:18)*. That is why Paul prays:

"that He would grant you, according to the riches of His glory, to be strengthened with might through His Spirit in the inner man, 17 that Christ may dwell in your hearts through faith; **that you, being rooted and grounded in love, 18 may be able to comprehend with all the saints what is the width and length and depth and height - 19 to know the love of Christ which passes knowledge;** *that you may be filled with all the fullness of God."* *(Eph 3:16-19)*

When we begin to comprehend His immense, incomprehensible love, we open up to receive of His fullness. That is what brings transformation. Paul elsewhere says that nothing – absolutely nothing, nor anyone, can ever separate us from His love:

143

*"Who shall separate us from the love of Christ? Shall tribulation, or distress, or persecution, or famine, or nakedness, or peril, or sword? 36 As it is written: 'For Your sake we are killed all day long; We are accounted as sheep for the slaughter.' 37 Yet in all these things we are more than conquerors through Him who loved us. 38 For I am persuaded that neither death nor life, nor angels nor principalities nor powers, nor things present nor things to come, 39 nor height nor depth, **nor any other created thing, shall be able to separate us from the love of God which is in Christ Jesus our Lord.**" (Rom 8:35-39)*

It is impossible to be persuaded of God's inescapable love, as Paul here describes, and still have a stronghold of fear and doubt concerning God's love for you. The enemy usually speaks to us in the first person, but we are not to be ignorant of His devices. When he comes and whispers in your ear: "God doesn't love me," do not receive it into your heart, but rather do what Jesus did when the tempter came to tempt Him. Tell him the truth: *"be gone Satan. For it is written: No created thing shall be able to separate me from the love of God in Jesus Christ my Lord." "God is love and there are no 'ifs' or 'buts' about it."* We have been given authority over all the power of the enemy. Resist the enemy with the truth as it is in Christ and he will flee from you.

Satan is a liar and his strongholds are all built upon lies we have believed and received in our hearts. Now simply believe and receive the truth which shall make you free. Don't try to use carnal weapons against spiritual strongholds. Continue rebuking his lies with the truth concerning God's unfailing love for you and this stronghold will be demolished, setting you free to obey Christ, empowered by the knowledge of His love, rather than trying to obey in your flesh, crippled by debilitating fear and insecurity.

Lie: "I am an unworthy sinner."

Many Christians are convinced that, even after being sanctified, justified and cleansed by the blood of Jesus, they are still nothing more than unworthy sinners. They claim that the only difference between who they were and who they now are is that they are now sinners saved by grace. Yet, the only text they can use to argue this point does not say what it seems to say when seen in its context. Paul said:

144

*"This is a faithful saying and worthy of all acceptance, that **Christin Jesus came into the world to save sinners, of whom I am chief.**" (1Tim 1:15)*

They point to this text and say: *"See, Paul himself declares, 'I am' (present tense) a sinner."* While it is true that Paul here says, not only that he was a sinner but also *"the chief of sinners,"* the context clearly indicates that he is not referring to his present condition, but rather to the title he held. The word translated *"chief"* is *protos* which in the context means *"in first place."* What Paul meant to say was, *"as far as sinners, I hold the title."* He is not talking about his present state but rather to the reputation he earned for himself in his former life as a Pharisee. This becomes clear when we see it in light of what he previously said in verse 13:

*"although **I WAS formerly** a **blasphemer**, a **persecutor**, and an **insolent** man; **BUT** I obtained mercy because I did it ignorantly in unbelief." (1Tim 1:13)*

Paul calls the believers saints 34 times, but not once does he call them sinners. He even calls the carnal Christians at Corinth, saints. Throughout the entire New Testament, the title, "sinners," is reserved for those who have not yet repented and been born again. Paul, on the contrary, says that we are now a new creation in Christ. He makes it clear to the Corinthians that if we are truly saved, we are no longer sinners:

*"Do you not know that the unrighteous will not inherit the kingdom of God? Do not be deceived. Neither fornicators, nor idolaters, nor adulterers, nor homosexuals, nor sodomites, 10 nor thieves, nor covetous, nor drunkards, nor revilers, nor extortioners will inherit the kingdom of God. 11 **And such WERE some of you. BUT you were washed, BUT you were sanctified, BUT you were justified** in the name of the Lord Jesus and by the Spirit of our God." (1Cor 6:9-11)*

When he confronted sin in the lives of the saints at Corinth he didn't say: *"stop sinning you sinners."* Instead he reminded them of who they now were in Christ:

*"**Do you not know** that you are the temple of God and that the Spirit of God dwells in you?" (1Cor 3:16)*

145

*"**Do you not know** that your bodies are members of Christ?"* (1Cor 6:15)

*"**Do you not know** that the saints will judge the world?" (1Cor 6:2)*

*"**Do you not know** that we shall judge angels?" (1Cor 6:3)*

*"**Do you not know** that your body is the temple of the Holy Spirit who is in you?" (1Cor 6:19)*

You see, the problem with the carnal Christian is not that he is a sinner, but rather that he is a saint who does not know who he really is in Christ. As my friend, pastor Alexander Veloza aptly illustrates, before we were in Christ it was in our very nature to sin, just as it is in a pig's nature to wallow in the mire. You can bathe a pig, dress him up in a nice suit with a bowtie and make him smell good with cologne, but as soon as you let him loose, he will go straight back to wallowing in the mire, because that is how he is by nature.

However, God's solution was not to dress up the old man and make him act contrary to who he is by nature. He gave us the Law to show us the futility of trying to reform and redirect our old man. God's solution is a new creation altogether. God's grace isn't simply His enabling a pig to act like something it is not. God's grace creates us anew with Christ's own life – making us partakers of God's divine nature. Now, we are no longer sinners but saints. We may still fall into sin, but it is no longer in our nature to stay there. Continuing with the above analogy, being born of God is like being instantly transformed from the pig (sinner) we were by nature, into a cat (saint). In a moment's time we were recreated in true righteousness and holiness *(Eph 4:24)*. While a pig loves to grovel in the mire, a cat hates it. If a cat sees a mud-hole, it doesn't go wallow in it. It carefully avoids even soiling its paws, and when it does soil its feet it licks them clean at the first opportunity.

A sinner sins and loves it but a saint, although he may fall into sin, loathes it. The lie that says to us in first person: *"I am nothing more than a wretched sinner saved by grace,"* is just another stronghold of the enemy, which must be confronted with the truth concerning who we now are as a new creation in Christ. If every time you soil your feet you feel bad and your inner voice says: *"I am a failure." "I am nothing more than a wretched sinner," "I am unworthy,"* that is an

146

indication that there is still a stronghold of the enemy's lie in your mind that needs to be verbally confronted with the truth as it is in Jesus Christ every time it presents itself, until the stronghold is completely demolished.

When you hear, *"I am an unworthy sinner"* in your mind, don't embrace it. Don't receive it as your own confession. The enemy's strategy is to speak to you in the first person, so you will receive it as if it were your own confession. Don't receive it. It may have the appearance of humility, but it is a lie. Declare instead the truth. Preach to the devil and he will flee from you because he cannot bear the truth. Confess the truth with your mouth: *"I am now the righteousness of God in Christ;" (Rom 3:22; 2Cor 5:21). "I am accepted (highly favored) in the Beloved;" (Eph 1:6). "There is now no more condemnation for me because I am in Christ Jesus." (Rom 8:1).* [16]

In order to effectively demolish the enemy's strongholds, we must avoid being governed by our emotions. If you are a new creature in Christ, the new normal is to feel bad when you sin, but feeling bad isn't in and of itself repentance, and feeling bad has no power to change your conduct as long as your thinking continues to be erroneous.

Repentance is *metanoéo,* a change in your thinking. Although it is now normal for you to feel bad when you sin, the enemy's strongholds cannot be destroyed by feeling bad but only by taking captive your thoughts to obey Christ. Truth transforms our minds before it affects our emotions. You can't feel your way into victory. You must first renew your mind, according to the truth as it is in Christ, taking captive every thought to the obedience of Christ. Once you know the truth and by faith consider it to be your new reality, then you can speak to the lies that have until now kept your will and your emotional life in bondage.

Whether or not something is true is not determined by how you feel. The truth is that God loves you, whether you feel it or not. You

---

[16] Since the older Greek manuscripts do not contain the final words *"...who do not walk according to the flesh, but according to the Spirit,"* most Greek scholars conclude that it was added later by a scribe. For that reason most recent translations simply read *"There is therefore now no condemnation to those who are in Christ Jesus."*

are valuable to God, whether you feel valuable or not. You are forgiven, whether you feel it or not. You are righteous and accepted before God, whether you feel it or not. Transformation comes through the renewing of our *minds*. Our emotional life may be in shambles due to a lifetime of rejection and abuse. It may take time for our emotions to heal and align themselves with the truth as it is in Jesus. But God has given us powerful weapons and as we learn to consistently use the sword of the Spirit and wear the helmet of salvation and the breastplate of faith, love, and the knowledge of our righteous standing in Christ, God will lead us from strength to strength; from victory to victory; from faith to faith; from glory to glory *(Eph 6:14-17; 1Thess 5:8)*.

Remember, our calling is not to become what we are not, but rather to awake to who we already are in Christ, and as we do that our lives will be transformed into His image.

But we all, with unveiled face,
beholding as in a mirror the glory of the Lord,
are being transformed into the same image from glory to glory,
just as by the Spirit of the Lord.
(2Cor 3:18)

Contact: http://www.triumphofmercy.com
Author: George Sidney Hurd

148

Made in the USA
Middletown, DE
06 March 2021

34950372R00090